Dressed For
VICTORY
PUTTING ON THE FULL
ARMOR OF GOD

Dr. William H. Curtis

DEDICATION

To my wife, Christine, and my daughter, Houston,
for the sacrifices you have made over all these years of ministry.

To Mt. Ararat, for providing a laboratory
for sermonic and ministry ideas and for trusting pastoral leadership.

William H. Curtis Ministries
271 Paulson Avenue
Pittsburgh, PA 15206

International Standard Book Number: 978-1-940786-23-0

Library of Congress Catalogue Card Number: Available Upon Request

Printed in the United States of America

Trademarks

Dressed For VICTORY
PUTTING ON THE FULL
ARMOR OF GOD

FOREWORD

There is no doubt that we are in a war. Though our government would identify political forces and the captains of industry would point out economic enemies, people of faith understand who is really giving guidance to the disturbing realities each of us face. Most of our time and attention is consumed with the struggle and little attention is given to the architect of our despair. Dr. William Curtis takes time to talk about the enemy in the enemy's Achilles' heel.

It is time for the church and for Christians to take charge of their destiny and fight the "behind the scenes" forces that are attempting to thwart our mission and our living. This work is such an attempt. I am strengthened by the scholarly yet folksy way that Dr. Curtis empowers each of us to believe and fight the good fight of faith. The enemy convinces us that we are fighting people and individuals, but this work unmasks the hand of the true enemy and his intent.

For years we have heard about the armor we have; yet we have still felt the sting—the whip—upon our lives while being penned to the mat. For many, the armor was just a statement, not a reality. Reading these pages will change all of that. The armor will come alive, faith will come alive, and courage will come alive. This book is for those who have concluded that defeat is no longer an option. You have to win and you will win.

Each piece of armor has meaning and power for the believer, and you will discover that as you glean insight after insight reading through these pages.

Dr. William Curtis is a profound thinker and preacher. His years of theological thinking and pastoral ministry have made him keenly aware of the struggles we face, and the power of God that is available, to empower us. This is a truly "Guide for the Dauntless." Warfare is a science and soldiers have to understand their enemy and understand how to fight that enemy.

He has taken time to hear the voice of God and has cultivated the skills necessary to communicate that word. God had this book written for you. Maximize its message by living and winning the battles you have to face. The war is already won because you and I are dressed in the "Armor of God!"

— Bishop Walter Scott Thomas, Sr.
Senior Pastor, *New Psalmist Baptist Church*

ONE:

LEARNING TO LIVE STRONG

Ephesians 6:10-11

"¹⁰Finally, be strong in the Lord and in his mighty power. ¹¹Put on the full armor of God, so that you can take your stand against the devil's scheme." (NIV)

The New Living Translation says:

"¹⁰A final word: Be strong in the Lord and in his mighty power. ¹¹Put on all of God's armor so that you will be able to stand firm against all strategies of the devil."

The Expanded Translation of the New Testament captures it this way:

"¹⁰Finally, be constantly strengthened in the Lord and in the active efficacy of the might that is inherent in Him. ¹¹Clothe yourself with the full armor of God to the end that you will be able to hold your ground against the strategies of the devil."

WHAT DOES IT MEAN TO "LIVE STRONG"?

In our modern world, we hear the term "live strong" all the time. We often associate it with being committed to an athletic or fitness accomplishment. Sometimes, our mind will make the jump to living strong for our family or our kids—taking this "I can do this" mentality into our work environment or our personal lives. But, do we "live strong" all the time? Do we even know what that means? Certainly, one person's definition of the term or phrase is different than another's. In some world's, living strong is being fit, eating right, rising up the corporate ladder, or getting your kids into the right school. In other worlds, living strong means just surviving—getting food on the table, avoiding illness, taking odd jobs to make some money, or getting back on track after a lifetime of mistakes or problems. All in all, we always have to be ready for when we are tested in any way—in any capacity. Life will show us many enemies, and we need to have the fortitude to stand up to them.

The answer to why the apostle Paul wants us to live strong is very simple. He wants us to live strong because the enemy is working a strategy of attack against us. The New International Version of the Bible calls it a scheme. This particular strategy of attack that the enemy is working is tailored to do several things—in this story—and in your daily lives, whether you recognize it or not:

One, the enemy's strategy in your life is to cloud your judgment or corrupt your thinking. In our lives, we've all fallen prey to friends who coerce us to do something against our better judgment. Or, we've been involved in relationships and, suddenly, find that our lifestyle is one we no longer recognize. These situations never make us happy, but they are often hard to notice and/or difficult to leave behind or change. After all, once these impressions have been made, then the enemy—in the form of bad behavior, bad influences, or distraction—is hard to turn away.

In our lives, we've all fallen prey to friends who coerce us to do something against our better judgment.

Second, the enemy's strategy is to injure your heart so as to corrupt your emotions. And, again, once we are in these situations—maybe we've been made to feel guilty or obligated AND, once we're in these predicaments, we often start to feel badly about ourselves and question our own judgment—and we can't get out. We feel sorry for our abuser or we feel sorry for ourselves, and the situation just gets worse.

Third, the enemy's strategy is to weaken your defenses to increase your vulnerabilities. Certainly, we've all had these issues—enablers who want us to continue bad behavior—influencers who want us to move onto worse lifestyle choices—and/or those who just want to put us down or make us feel bad daily.

The enemy's strategy is to make us all unable to be effective at advancing or making any positive progress in life—at work, in our personal lives, or in our spiritual lives. The enemy's strategy is also to connect you to a life of falsity—one that, as we mentioned before, we don't recognize anymore as we head down those destructive paths shown to us by those who do not have our best interests at heart. The enemy's strategy, finally, is to lure you onto a destructive path. And, this is just not arbitrary prose; each of these issues are listed here because they are to be countered by what Paul says and what we should learn from Paul—from our daily worship—from ourselves and others with positive influence. Further, Paul tells us cloth ourselves with this way of thinking—these protective thoughts and practices.

Since the enemy is going to attack your ability to think and process rational thoughts in a way will, potentially, keep us centered in the perfect will of God, Paul is going to suggest that you put on the helmet of salvation. That "helmet" or way of thinking is designed to protect the mind. Paul encourages that there is a spiritual response to every demonic attack. What I want you to grasp is the fact that Paul says what the enemy is working is a strategy, a scheme, a methodeia (Greek) or a method in which Satan and all his influences lie in wait to work his cunning arts of deception and destruction into your life. Make no mistake—it is a method, a strategy and a scheme. The methods of Satan and the other evil influences that we encounter daily is used to deceive, in this story, a disciple—in daily life, the rest of us. Do not underestimate the enemy's ability to deceive!

We don't always want to hear that the enemy is already acting in our daily lives—that the influences that we've allowed are not always the best. Of course, this is the enemy at work—having developed an art form for this type of attack and temptation—ultimately, no matter who or what that negative influence is, it will make us all self-destruct or reach an irretrievable abyss from which it would be hard to return.

The enemy's method involves chaos, temptations, tricks, traps, attacks, invasions, and false images. No matter the cause—no matter the source, it will come as a planned deception to spiritually turn us away from what is good in our lives. Easy money—easy success—easy life—NEVER come easily. If the enemy leads you to believe otherwise, that helmet of salvation is what you need to focus on to return to a spiritual, honest, and, yes, successful life.

The enemy's method involves chaos, temptations, tricks, traps, attacks, invasions, and false images.

Now, in our text here, Paul says that we should not deal with the enemy by fighting the enemy. Paul is suggesting to us, in chapter six of this Bible verse, that we deal with the enemy by living strong in the Lord. The enemy is not changing his method of attack in our lives, and the enemy knows his method works, especially for people who don't do what Paul suggests. Trying to fight the enemy in response to a strategy employed before we were even born will be a futile attempt at best. The enemy doesn't use these strategies, methods, schemes, or agendas because he has little confidence in their effectiveness. The enemy has chosen his planned attack for your life—all of our lives—because he knows it works. It has worked in past generations. It is working in our present generation and, as much as we don't want to confess or admit it, it will continue to work in succeeding generations. The same problems plague our families, communities, and the world in each generation. Good people fall prey to bad things. The saying "bad things happen to good people" is common, because it is true, in part. What we need to explore is how or why we allow ourselves to become victim to such problems—and how we, and others, can slip deeper into the grips of Satan and his traps. Abuse, drugs, money problems, chronic illness—all of them terrible; some of them preventable. We need to learn to offset what we can. Living strong is all part of this.

Good people fall prey to bad things.

I know many of us will hear Paul's words and be convinced that we are one of those special Christians—super Christians who can win by a different method or win by a different response. However, I need to remind everyone that, over time and for many years, Christians who have been as close to God as we are—as useful to God as we are—as effective in kingdom service as we are—have fallen when they have abandoned the method Paul is suggesting. There is no other method for your survival in life but to grow stronger in the Lord—to LIVE STRONG—in whatever capacity that means to you. Paul suggests the best response to whatever the enemy is attempting to do is for you to grow stronger in the Lord, so that every time the enemy attacks, you grow stronger. And what does this mean, really, to us? Do we go to church on Sunday? Yes. Do we minister to our communities when we can? Yes. Do we care for and love our families? Yes. Do we do the best we can in school or work, testing ourselves and using discipline to grow and become successful? Yes.

Whenever the enemy gets busy, we must counter the enemy's activity by our spiritual maturity.

Whenever the enemy gets busy, we must counter the enemy's activity by our spiritual maturity. The place of concentration, therefore, is not on the attack; the focus is not on the enemy. The focus is not to become introverted, victimized, or intimidated. The place of concentration and the place of focus are on living stronger in the Lord.

Truly living strong is hard, and I get concerned when I hear people who end their prayers or address a portion of their prayers to the devil—

as if we are frightened or intimidated—as if he has some power over us. My suggestion is always to not waste any prayer time talking to the devil. To talk to him is to acknowledge that we are remotely concerned about his presence. When the enemy is around and when the enemy is busy, we must not focus on the enemy. Remember to focus on living stronger in the Lord.

This is not always natural or easy to do, as I said earlier. This is evident because Paul had to teach it to the saints. The Lord knows it is not easy for us, so He left the teaching in biblical record for us. If we see that even the saints and those we respect in hindsight (those who history tells us are great, strong people) had trouble heeding his warning and taking his advice, then maybe we will take it more seriously. How hard is it to stay and live strong? How hard is it to set your path and not stray unless it is to improve and become better? It is harder than we all think. We stray all the time. And, the reason it's not easy is because to watch the devil present himself in a specific area of your life (bringing to that area his tricks, his traps, his methods, his schemes, and his strategies) and then watch that area of your life become affected creates such a helpless feeling. Many times, we are weakened further at the thought of letting the devil get to us—letting the bad things in life take hold. And remember, the temptation is to want to fight him—to go right after him in response to the anger we feel regarding his uninvited presence in our lives. The natural response is to concentrate on the area that Satan is attacking—to look at what he is doing and to pay attention to the affect it is having on us. Concentrating on this area makes us want to try to fix it, secure it, or respond to it. In this way, we lose focus; we forget about what is important, and we lose sight of that path to success and a spiritual and rewarding life. Again, Paul is teaching us to, instead, make our responses to grow stronger in the Lord. He is teaching us to become more disciplined, more spiritual, more enlightened and educated in light of the truth we know and the falsehoods trying to tempt us. And, we should know the difference; we should know when we feel unhappy or tempted or out of control, but we don't always see it right away.

The questions are always the same: How do I accomplish this and what does it mean in the long run? How do I learn to live strong in the Lord's mighty power? We need to do so by, first, accepting that the answer to every attack in my life is to strengthen our capabilities through increased pursuit of the Lord. Be strong in the Lord! One translation writes it this way, "Be made capable in Him." Another translation says, "Receive strength from Him."

Be strong in the Lord!

And, here's where faith comes into play. Because, this "be strong" in the Greek really says "be being strong." We can interpret this to mean, in part, that I can't be strong today for tomorrow. I'm strong today—and I feel strong and ready—accomplished in what I need to do, but...tomorrow I'm going to need to continue being strong because the enemy's attack today may bring a new method tomorrow, and we all have to be ready. We may think, "If I've conquered the strategy for today, I need to continue to be (being) strong so that I don't win today and take a loss tomorrow." We need to maintain our strength—learn from our challenges—and practice vigilance, strength, and faith every day.

I learn to live strong in the Lord by exercising enough faith to feel confident that all evidence of the enemy's method being worked in my life will be met by an increased ability given to me by God. My faith gives me the confidence I need so that when the enemy releases a fresh attack for the working of his overall strategy, I already know that the Lord is giving me necessary ability to stand up in the attack. You don't have to panic. You don't have to retreat. You don't have to surrender. You don't have to give up. You don't have to be depressed. Whenever Satan gets active and busy, the Lord makes you able to stand up in it. HE makes you strong. My strength comes because God knows that Satan is planning to work his strategy, and when I get up in the morning, God already knows what the devil is trying to do. He makes you able to stand up. The Lord makes you strong.

Whenever Satan gets active and busy, the Lord makes you able to stand up in it.

You have to believe in faith that you are strong enough in Him to handle every attack even when you don't know from where it will be launched. Even when I don't know from which human vessel or agency I may get my next challenge, I do believe that the Lord will make me strong enough to overcome it. The challenge is not to panic. If I can be "being strong," I can maximize my present strength for my current attack. But when the enemy in his newest strategy brings a fresh attack (and it will happen as Paul has established), I have time to be "being strong" for that. I can take a breath and draw on my fortitude to get through it. When the attack comes, I have a choice regarding how I will respond to the attack. I can choose to get angry. I can choose to match carnal weapons used against me with carnal weapons attempted back at the enemy. I can seek security in people. I can take it out on people that have nothing to do with that attack being launched in my life. I have time to make a choice. Or I can choose that the attack is a signal that it is time to grow.

The enemy being busy is a signal that it's time for me to grow stronger in the Lord. If the enemy is not attacking you fresh, it is only because he has no fear of you doing any damage to his strategy. If you are a threat to his agenda, then he is on your tracks. Paul says next time we are under the enemy's attack—to SHOUT. His active presence is a demonstration that you are on a pathway to spiritual maturity. Your job is to not panic before you grow. Grow first and then you'll look back and see that what the enemy meant for evil, God used it for your good. Don't look at the strength and energy and effort that you have right now. Look at the necessary grace of God. God will give sufficient grace for your season's situation. Simply stated, when the enemy is attacking, God will give you what you need to stand up in it. You have to go into the attack believing it.

Grow first and then you'll look back and see that what the enemy meant for evil, God used it for your good.

Further, we all learn to live strong by preplanning exactly what our responses will be. For example, while watching the Outdoor Channel

(Television, Cable Programming), I happened upon a show about creating a home and a planning against a home invasion. I became fascinated with the host saying that the first response to a home invasion is to have already devised a plan that can be deployed at that fearful moment. Because, when under pressure, if you don't already have a plan, you will hurt yourself trying not to get hurt. The host said that the first thing you need to do is make the home harder to get into. Secondly, you must have response weapons accessible and spread throughout the house. He said to design a room to be what you call your "safe room." Put a special door on your safe room with the hinges on the inside rather than the outside. Have in that room a cell phone that is constantly charged and ready to go. He said if an intruder should invade your home and you run into your safe room, as the intruder is approaching your room, start yelling a name. Even if no one is in the house, start calling a specific name. He said that since a name has been called, the invader will run for fear of the name. And…in this moment in my life, watching this show, evaluating my circumstances and checking my readiness, I realized that it was a great analogy for our readiness for an attack from Satan. What's wrong with creating a "safe room" in our minds? What's wrong with knowing a name to call—the Lord—when we need help? What is wrong with being ready? Nothing!

What God is trying to say to us is invaders do come. In fact, Satan has a strategy to break into your safe house. Don't be full of anxiety, because if Satan breaks into your safe house, you go to your safe place. Lock the door and have charged a method of communication so you can call 911 dispatch for some help—whatever that 911 may be—whatever your "go to" help may be in these situations. And, if you hear the footsteps of the enemy approaching your safe room, start calling a name. Start calling the name Jesus! The enemy flees at the name of Jesus! We know this; we just have to execute our plans.

The question is: Have you determined what your response will be when the enemy attacks? If your answer is that you don't have a preplanned agenda, then doesn't that explain why when the enemy attacks your life, you start acting like you don't know what to do and things get worse? When the enemy attacks you, because you don't have a preplan, you respond by acting out of control—not yourself. Instead, make a decision now to place spiritual weapons around your life so that wherever you have to mentally hide, you have something to help you feel secure. Make that hiding place somewhere you're able to barricade yourself in—keep to your own strengths and not let anyone stray you—thereby, keeping the enemy or any negative influences away. Paul tells us that, for him, it was the 'secret place of the most high God under the shadow of the almighty.' We must get in God's secret place and walk under His shadow, and we'll have no need to fear regarding what the enemy is trying to do in our lives. Paul said "Put on the whole armor of God that you might be able to stand against the schemes of the devil:" Helmet of salvation, breast plate of righteousness, shield of faith, sword of the spirit, loins gird with truth, and feet shod with the preparation of the gospel of peace. Don't concentrate on the specifics of the uniform, because every word in scripture is important. We don't shout because we have clothing to put on. Our first responsibility is to put it on. Put on in the Greek is transliterated "sink into it." It means, "sink into" your clothing. What kind of clothing? Paul says it is armor. The armor is for defense, and it is to cover the head to the toe, the mind to the direction, and the thinking to the action. The Lord will do the protecting, but you have to do the putting on. What we want God to do is show up and stay to protect. God says put on, and when He shows up He'll protect. It works once you put it on. In fact, I guarantee you it will work, but you have to put it on.

We must get in God's secret place and walk under His shadow.

Look at the metaphor Paul paints for us. He, like us, is a victim of his present context. Where is Paul writing this? He's writing it from prison. He could have used other illustrative, linguistic material to describe what we need to be clothed in, but he uses the guard's uniform, the soldier's uniform because he is reading based on his context. In Paul's day when you are locked up, you were chained to the guard. Paul is chained to his guard, looking at his uniform. He observes the guard's weapons. He sees the guard's shield. He can see the guard's helmet. He observes the guard's belt. He can see the guard's breastplate. He looks at the guard's sandals. And he realizes that while he and the guard are different and while he and the guard are opposed, both are dressed the same. Paul says the guard is dressed naturally, but "I was dressed spiritually." Paul says as he looked at the guard, he got a revelation. He got the revelation that he needed to tell the saints that, "Just as the guard is dressed in the natural, you need to be dressed in the spiritual." That's why he said put on the helmet of salvation, the breastplate of righteousness, the shield of faith the sword of the spirit, your loins gird with truth, your feet shod with the preparation of the gospel of peace. He says don't put on one piece unless you are going to put on every piece. Put on the whole armor of God. It is useless to put the helmet on and leave the breastplate off, because all that says to the enemy is don't shoot at your mind but shoot at your heart. Don't leave the sword but take up the shield, because if you're going to extinguish fiery darts you have to be ready to cut between bone and marrow.

In 1996, there was a Bible created, marketed to Christians, the manufacturer designed what they called a "Bulletproof Bible" that was marketed to be placed in the inside pocket just over the heart. That Bible was unique, because it was layered with anti-ballistic material. The manufacturer marketed this Bible that it will protect because it was layered with anti-ballistic material. The problem was that the Bible was only able to withstand a .38 caliber bullet, and if the bullet coming at you was a bullet stronger than a .38, then you would not be protected by the Word. The question is: Why couldn't the manufacturer create a Bible strong enough to withstand any size bullet coming its way? It's because the Word was not designed to be worn for protection. The Word was designed to be internalized for protection. When it's worn on the outside, there are some weapons that will penetrate that "armor." But, when the Word gets on the inside (when the armor is strong there) the Bible says that no weapon formed against me shall prosper. We are a culture of Bible carriers, but we are not yet a culture of Bible bearers. And, if we can get some people to bear the Bible and internalize it—make it part of their spiritual growth and strength—rather than carry the Bible and simply say they believe or they are ready, we can survive some of our attacks.

This is why Paul says that, after you clothe yourself in the full armor of God, you've got to stand and show your faith. Well, how can you do that? Remember—no disciple should ever be found running from the devil. Every disciple ought to stand in the power and strength of their relationship with Jesus Christ.

TWO:

BECOMING MORE EFFICIENT AND POWERFUL IN WORSHIP

Ephesians 6:14[a]

"Stand firm then with the belt of truth buckled around your waist…" *(NIV)*

WHAT CAN WE LEARN FROM THE BELT OF TRUTH?

Truth is often a liquid concept. To many, personal truths are always changing as people evolve and develop new interests, become more educated, or go through periods of enlightenment and change. For others, deep, personal truths never change; their faith remains unwavering, their personal habits never change, and they are, for the most part, reliable "set in their ways" types who will always have a solid sense of self.

Chained to the wrist of the Roman soldier guarding him, Paul is fighting to stay focused on Jesus. He is in the face of death, looking for ways to keep his mind on things that would help saints grow in difficult times. Paul is fixated on the armor the guard is wearing, and he starts to draw parallels between what that solider is wearing and what a Christian needs to wear, in order to live a strong life and to put up a good fight of faith. Paul knows that just as the soldier dresses for what may be a confrontation with an opposing force, the Christian, too, should expect that there is a strong possibility that a determined foe is going to attack in such a way that a Christian would have no choice but to fight if they want to live strong in the faith.

Paul can clearly see the sword and the shield of the soldier. Both are impressive. Both are critical for putting up a good fight. Paul sees the helmet; he sees the shoes, and he knows of their importance and significance as well. The apostle Paul also knows that everything that the soldier needs to live strong requires that the soldier wraps first, around his loose fitting garment, a belt or a sash. That belt prevents what is loosely connected from restricting mobility. That belt provides something sturdy upon which to hang the heavy, but needed, sword. Without that belt, the soldier is not as mobile, flexible, or confident of the moves he may need to make. He won't be as agile. He will not have the freedom of mobility, because he has nothing to hang the heavy stuff on. That means the soldier will have to carry the heavy stuff in his hands. Since he always has to carry everything in his hands, he will fatigue quickly. He moves with fewer options. He can't be as strong as he could be if he had something sturdy he could hang some heavy stuff on.

Paul sees that belt and starts thinking to himself that—just like the soldier first puts on his belt to start dressing in his physical armor, so, too, the Christian must put on a belt of spirituality, to start dressing in his or her spiritual armor. For Paul, this essential first piece to living strong in the Lord's mighty power—the first piece to making a strong stand against the enemy—is to put on a belt of truth. And, it should be this way for us too. Even when we waver or change our point of view in politics or lifestyle, our faith needs to stay strong—our spirituality needs to stay protected.

For Paul, this locked up but liberated apostle, it's easy to see why people are losing spiritual battles. For Paul, it's easy to see why saints are losing the fight of faith against this determined foe. It's because many people attempting to fight have not wrapped themselves in truth or have not wrapped themselves in enough truth to remain positively mobile, significantly agile, spiritually committed, and mentally determined. Paul surmises they are saints not wrapped tightly in the belt of truth. They are easy targets for the enemy, because there is none, or not enough, truth wrapped around them. Because they have not enough truth wrapped around them, they are forced to carry the heavy stuff, the heavy promises of the word of God. These must be carried if a saint is going to live strong in the Lord's mighty power.

Many people attempting to fight have not wrapped themselves in truth.

And we all know what I'm referring to here, because we all run into some "beltless" people on a daily basis. We've all observed, been in conversation with, or even voluntarily hung around some beltless people. It is easy to tell that they are beltless because, when they start talking, they get injured so easily. They are defensive, argumentative, and often hard to talk to. There is not enough truth wrapped around them; they don't feel secure or protected. Beltless people believe everything said to them, believe everything said about them, and believe everything said about others. They can easily be persuaded to trade convictions for convenience and service for entitlement. Their minds, moods, and motivations change almost like folk change clothes every day. They are for one thing today, against it tomorrow. They like you today but don't like you tomorrow. We all know them—maybe we've been one ourselves at one time. In hindsight, can we remember a time during which we didn't feel grounded spiritually or personally? Maybe something in our lives caused us to feel this way, and it took some praying and some deep introspection to get back on track. It was and will always be imperative that we do get back on track, though. There are so many challenges for us in life; it is best to have our belts of truth securely in place.

We've all observed, been in conversation with, or even voluntarily hung around some beltless people.

The enemy knows who is living and moving beltless, and he attacks their loose fitting identities, and their loose fitting personalities. He gets them to believe what isn't true about themselves until they do what reflects the lie they have been living—the untruths they have been subjected to, and, soon, their lives are out of control. We all need to be careful of this. We cannot live and talk one way and expect to be treated another. We've all heard of self-fulfilling prophecies—how people will expect themselves to fail and then they do fail. By contrast, there are people who expect success and live to make that happen. Therefore, they achieve what they want to—feats of which they are capable and, further, believe in and practice every day—through faith, discipline, and wearing their own belts of truth.

*The enemy knows who is living and moving beltless,
and he attacks their loose fitting identities,
and their loose fitting personalities.*

Paul knows we can live with these falsehoods, but we can't live strong that way. There is a way to live stronger. To start, Paul suggests, we consciously decide to put on our belts of truth. Strong living starts when we wrap strong beliefs around our lives. If we want to grow even stronger—if we want to be stronger Christians—if we want to experience deliverance from an unfulfilled life—if we want to be more effective and powerful in ministry and in everything we do, we all need more truth in our lives. More truth means more promises. More truth means more possibilities. More truth means wider vision. In other words, we can achieve great things—what we were meant for in this world—if we live strong by our belts of truth—our spiritual and personal strengths—never wavering, never allowing the enemy and his influences to sway us.

These might be simple statements and may even seem obvious, but I'll risk the simplicity to argue the profundity of the truth it is intended to reveal. Many people don't live strong, because many people don't believe their own strengths. To live strong, we all have to believe strong and wrap ourselves in the truth of who God is to us—to wrap ourselves in the truth of what God can do for us and with us—and to wrap ourselves in the truth of our abilities when we truly get to know Him. This is what turns our prayers from habit to weapon, from habit to tool, and from habit to resource. We are successful when we can see our potential and live strong to achieve it.

Many people don't live strong, because many people don't believe their own strengths.

I don't pray because it's a habit, and I encourage the rest of you to begin thinking that way too. My prayers are habitual, and I make them part of my daily spiritual life. But, I don't pray because it's a habit! I pray because I'm wrapped in the truth that God hears prayers, that God answers prayers, and that prayer changes people. We pray because somewhere along the course of our journey, we became full of enough conviction to believe that prayer changes people, and that prayer, in turn, changes things for us. We believe that God is God enough to be the best option to rest what's on my mind, whatever is on my mind.

Here is the question raised relative to the text: Is God, today, your absolute truth or is God expected to compete with equal pillars of truth you have placed at the table? Is God the sole source of ultimate truth or must God defend what He is portraying as truth against other truths you have lifted equal to a sovereign God? Is God truth enough in your life that when looking at evidence contrary to the word of God, you will anchor your hope on the word of God, even if the evidence doesn't change? Is God truth enough that when the door is closed, that doesn't mean it's closed to you? Is God truth enough for you that you will rest your convictions on the fact that when man locks, God can pick, and what man prevents, God can promote? Is God such absolute truth that just because you lose your job it doesn't mean you have to lose your joy and just because your money is not flowing in abundance it doesn't mean that God can't supply your every need? Just because the doctor says more tests need to be run, your truth says "by his stripes I am healed." When the enemy is encircling you like a flood, is God enough truth that you can declare the Lord will lift up a standard against him and prepare a table? Is God truth enough that when you look at clouds you can still have joy, because the sun shining on the inside is the S-o-n when you can't see the s-u-n?

Is God truth enough that when the door is closed, that doesn't mean it's closed to you?

To use another Biblical text, this one line in Sarah and Abraham's lives speaks to this very concept: "Against all hope, Abraham believed." All the evidence said "no," but God said "yes." In your life, does God always need to confirm what He says by what He shows? In order for you to believe it, do you always have to see it? Can you get to the place you need to go even if you don't see it? Yes, we all can.

Paul says everything else you carry will be maximized by how strong the belt of truth is wrapped around your waist. So when progress is minimized, can you hang it on the belt of truth that is strong enough, wrapped tight enough, that you will believe God no matter what, you'll trust God no matter what, you'll wait on God no matter what, and you'll keep talking based on what He is saying, no matter what?

In this portion of scripture, Paul is not talking about the belt of truth speaking in peaceful and serene times. To have integrity with the context, Paul, in this portion, is talking about our response to spiritual warfare. Paul says that we're, in essence, wrestling. The enemy is attempting to throw us so as to pin all of us, who are not prepared, in embarrassing submission. Paul says he's doing it with schemes and tricks. Some translations put it as the "wiles of the devil." Paul says you combat it by first wrapping yourself tightly in truth, because the schemes will grip you where truth is absent from you.

It is clear that some of us are wrapped in something other than truth. For you to define your life counter to what the Word says and believe that it can ever be that bad—that it is too late—that nothing can change—that everything won't turn around—that it's, basically, all over—then, you have a belt on, but it isn't the belt of truth. Many of us parents know this, because when our teenagers come downstairs without a belt on, we know it. You know it by how they are walking. They walk like what's connected to them will easily fall off of them, and they can't carry what they should because they're trying to keep tight what's too loose. We can tell that they don't have a belt on, because they are walking trying to protect what's loose from falling off. Conscientious parents know that in order to give their child agility and mobility, and freedom and liberation of movement, we are telling them to put a belt on! Too many of us are walking around with too loose a theology, too loose a philosophy, and too loose an understanding of the Word of God. Put on the belt and tighten up your ideology, tighten up your philosophy, and tighten up your theology, so you can speak those things which are not as though they are and use His word to chart your future.

Too many of us are walking around with too loose a theology, too loose a philosophy, and too loose an understanding of the Word of God.

Henry Nouwen, A Dutch-born Catholic priest, spiritual advisor, and author, talks about how "we base our lives unfortunately on what we have, what we do, and what other people think about us." He says, to paraphrase, that we look back when we get older and we point to our trophies and say, "See, I had value." Nouwen goes on to say that all three of these aforementioned ways of defining ourselves are wrong. Instead, the only truth that brings definition to every person is this: "We are God's beloved daughters and sons. And it doth not yet appear what we shall be." You can work your whole life to have an identity based on materialism and lose it in one season of economic decline. You can base it on your beauty and wake up one day with one spot that turns into a battle with a disease that has been lying dormant, now alive and arrogant. You can base it on your relationships and wake up tomorrow and discover the person you once knew you no longer know. When it is all said and done, the one truth you can hang your future on is this, you are God's child and God takes care of His children. God's got a plan for you and his plan is glorious for your future.

Paul, when talking about the belt of truth, is not just talking about the accumulation of facts and not just growing smart about the truth of who God is, because truth as only facts will never help you fight the enemy. You don't fight the enemy with just facts, because the enemy knows more facts than you do. Remember—when Jesus is in his conversation being tempted in the wilderness, and it is the enemy that says, "Doesn't God say?" He knows the facts; he knows how to get to us—how to even get to Jesus. The issue is if the enemy can get you to base your religion just on facts, it will be like having a weapon, but one that you are not sure about how it will work or that you just don't know how to use. The two are different; truth and knowledge go hand in hand, but you need to know where you stand with your belt of truth—your knowledge base—all the time. You have to go from facts to conviction. Facts say God is God because a book says it. Conviction says God is God because I've seen Him in His sovereignty work. Facts are what David starts with when he responds to Goliath. "I have killed the lion and the bear." That's a fact. Conviction says, "And the Lord shall deliver you into my hands." Facts say our economy is bad. Conviction says God is still preparing tables. The facts say your background should have cancelled out your opportunities. Conviction says if God can use Abraham, David, Moses, Isaiah, Jeremiah, Ezekiel, Daniel, Shadrach, Meshach, Abednego, Peter, James, John, Paul, Silas, Mark, and Barnabas, then why not me! Fact is you don't have a car. Conviction is you are not stuck. None of us are ever stuck, and if we just try to show our conviction—try to live with discipline—try to keep that belt of truth close, then…we will see results.

You don't fight the enemy with just facts, because the enemy knows more facts than you do.

When Satan comes to Jesus in the wilderness and tempts Him, Jesus does not respond to Satan just by facts. He is experiencing and expressing convictions. When you are pressed, you always rehearse what you believe. We can tell what is tightly wrapped around you when your back is up against the wall. Paul is stating the next part of spiritual maturation is to learn how to live strong by letting you know what you know about God become convictions until you fight based on your convictions, not just your facts.

An Italian entrepreneur named Claudio Ciaravolo talks about what happened to him at an intersection of his own history when the law enforcers strictly enforced a seatbelt law. While he accepted the new seatbelt law, he didn't agree with it. Because he didn't agree with it, he had enough money to do something to promote his disagreement. He used his money to get a manufacturer to create a white business shirt with a black stripe that looked like a seatbelt across the shirt. His idea was that if a driver passed a police officer, the officer would see the stripe and misinterpret it as a seatbelt. The problem is that while he did escape the police officers, he could not save himself from a head on collision. To save himself from a crash he needed acceptance and agreement. Some of us are using God's Word to find out what the law says but then we leave and create a garment as if to presuppose we can fool God and make Him believe we've got the seatbelt of His Word strapped tightly around us. We are not hurting God but hurting ourselves. It's evident what is really wrapped around you once you crash into something and can't survive. Paul is clear that the belt of truth is an agreement with the total sufficiency of God alone.

Muhammad Ali was on a plane and was asked by the flight attendant to buckle his seatbelt in preparation for the flight. Ali replied, "Superman doesn't wear a seatbelt." The flight attendant looked at him and said, "Mr. Ali, that might be true but superman doesn't need a plane." The truth is put the seatbelt on!

FIRST INSTALLMENT:

A TESTIMONIAL TO THE ARMOR OF GOD

In life, we don't always feel like we are tested appropriately regarding our faith. Sometimes, we are asked if we are faithful—or maybe we defend our religion or our stance on spirituality at a dinner party full of non-believers on occasion. But, do we ever really test ourselves or publicly become witness to a life as a faithful person with deep commitment to God?

A colleague of mine recently recounted a story to me—a story that I feel really illustrates true bravery in a time of need and at a moment when no one else would step up and act. In this case, it took fortitude, thinking outside the box, and the use of all that we discussed so far—our belts of truth, our commitment to nailing ourselves to a faithful stance, our formidable breastplates of righteousness for all to see, and above all, the overall ability to live strong in faith and in God. Again, rarely do we truly demonstrate this strength we the faithful have in common, but, in this case, it was so satisfying to hear.

My friend works in an office that he deems a bit on the hostile side. By that, he doesn't mean that everyone is hostile, but he does indicate to me on occasion that the environment is very competitive and, at times, cutthroat. He, himself, will get nervous at times when a project is behind or when co-workers vying for the same position or accolades on a recent project know he's away on vacation. Nevertheless, the office functioned normally and politely on a daily basis despite all the angst.

During the last holiday season, one of the employees, a single mother, was working hard on a project. When one of her children was diagnosed with a serious illness, she had to take time off to care for the child. As one of the top employees at the firm, she was envied by many for her position and the respect that she received from the higher up executives at the company. According to my friend, she was always polite and courteous to people and did impeccable work.

Once she was out of the office for about a week, relying on co-workers to continue their work on her project and working furiously from home when she wasn't in the hospital with her sick child, the other people in the office began to talk. Suddenly, this nice, hard-working woman was victim to all sorts of vicious gossip behind her back. They talked about the circumstances of her divorce, they acted as though she was never nice or personable to any of them, they began to question her work on the project, and they even accused her of embellishing her child's illness. Soon, the rumblings were reaching the ears of her superiors, and there was talk about letting her go. Some people, eager for her position, even went to the boss to complain about her in order to expedite her separation from the company. Others, who had heard that her child had taken a turn for the worse and who knew that she was still working hard to bring the project to a close, began to talk about how they had seen her and she looked thin—and that they were worried about her and her other children. No one, however, would come forward and publicly defend her.

Further, they wouldn't speak up to the people who really mattered and document the lies being spread about her.

My friend told me that this kept him up at night. Knowing that the superiors in this company did not play games and expected top results, he was a bit reluctant to endanger his own job by—first, admitting to knowing about the office gossip—and second, siding with someone who was clearly (but wrongly) on her way out the door. He had to provide for his family too and needed a stable job. He worried about the repercussions for him in the workplace, knowing that a happy workplace often created a happy home, and he didn't want to change his life at all or make things more difficult for his family in any way. He thought long and hard about his options.

One day, while walking on his lunch hour, he thought about his position of faith. He thought, specifically, about his commitment to that faith and how it made him feel strong. He thought, too, about his distaste for anything untruthful and damaging and how he made truth a part of his daily life. He thought, mostly, about how living strong and maintaining faith and strength helped him get a good-paying job to begin with and gave him the daily skills needed to provide for, love, and nurture his own family. He knew he had to do the right thing.

That day, he went to his superiors with printed proof of this co-workers continued workplace success. He remained professional and appropriate but did mention what was being said about her in the office. He even went further to suggest to his superiors that they begin a reward process for good work in the office and that they begin a team approach to projects that would allow others to grow. As he talked, he was a little surprised at his own tone and the firmness of his speech. He wasn't sure if he was overstepping his responsibilities at all or if his suggestions would be received well, but he did know that helping someone in need and trying to make everything a little better even for those who had strayed down the path of the unfaithful and caused damage to another were the right things to do.

His meeting went well but was met with a few days of silence following the initial get together. He was worried but, again, confident that he had done the right thing. I shouldn't even have to say here that he was rewarded with a promotion—that the office dynamic changed with administration implemented new and improved work processes and that the woman returned to her job, unscathed and with her child healthy again. I should only have to say that standing up, nailed to the strength of faith—in position to fight for what was right—living strong in the moment with the belt of truth and the breastplate of absolute, true righteousness to keep him on task, my friend did what was right and would continue similar behavior in his life. I do need to say, here, that more of us should do the same.

THREE:

PROTECTION AGAINST THE UNEXPECTED

Ephesians 6:14[b]

> *"…With the breastplate of righteousness in place…" (NIV)*

BREASTPLATE OF RIGHTEOUSNESS

In revisiting the text, we find Paul chained to a Roman soldier. Now, he is spiritually trained to see God in every situation. Though uncertain about his physical future, Paul does see the purpose, reason, and value in being in his current imprisoned context. Paul is convinced that God wants to show him something, wants to teach him something. Paul is trained to believe that there is no place, no situation, no circumstance, where God is not revealing Himself. Paul believes that if we live faith expectant then we can find the purpose of our place in life by finding God in the place where we find ourselves. Wherever we find ourselves, God is there! Paul knows that one of the things God wants to show him must be connected to this guard with whom he finds himself chained.

In our own lives, we often say that we understand why God has given us certain challenges, citing "that which doesn't kill us makes us stronger" when examining our own lives or offering advice like, "God only gives you what you can handle" to others who are suffering or going through challenging periods in life. Do we really get what it means to be "spiritually trained," however? Do we truly understand what we need to do when faced with difficult situations of faith or in other areas of our personal, emotional, or professional lives?

None of us are resistant to challenges in life. We all face them to the best of our abilities. It is notable, however, that all of our abilities are different. And—why is that? Is our training in faith so different? Is our perspective so different? Often, we get so caught up in our lives that we forget to protect ourselves from hidden challenges or aggressors. Our enemies aren't always as apparent as the co-worker who wants to take our job—or the person who is rude to us in the checkout line at the grocery store. Often, our aggressors, as discussed previously, are temptations or influences that may lead us from our path in life—away from family, self, and God. Our protection has to go beyond a general feeling that we are OK or ready to meet challenges. We have to consciously protect where we are vulnerable.

In our text, Paul starts to pay close attention to what the guard is wearing. He starts to pay attention, specifically, to the armor the guard is wearing. He sees the two bronze plates sewn into leather that form what Paul calls the breastplate. From the neck to the navel, the guard is covered in the front with this breastplate to protect him from any damaging attempts to pierce his body, perhaps puncturing vital organs that would rob the guard of his life and perhaps his future. Just as Paul looked at that sturdy belt around the waist of the soldier, which brought a tightening to an otherwise loose fitting clothing—and just as that sturdy belt upon which the soldier would hang the heavy but necessary sword—

Paul sees the breastplate and equates its importance with the importance of righteousness for the follower of Jesus Christ. In his mind, what else would protect the vital organs or vital core of any belief system—the life of any true Christian—but something that protects the very source of life in a person—a metal breastplate. In the case of our Christianity and our allegiance to God and to Jesus, this protection, to Paul, comes in the form of righteousness.

In the text, Paul thinks about what he shares, in that moment of epiphany, in instruction with the saints. He knows that the enemy is going to constantly attack the child of God. The enemy, Paul says (and as we've learned in previous chapters), is always attacking with schemes, strategies, and tricks with the aim being like a wrestler to toss the child of God to the mat or to pin the saints in embarrassed submission. Since we know this, Paul is trying to help the saints or the children of God live strong in the Lord's mighty power, particularly when attacked by the enemy's schemes. He knows that none of us can live strong against the enemy's schemes and tricks without the Lord's mighty power. He encourages a believer to become spiritually dressed right in order to put up a good fight and to stay secure and strong in the Lord.

First in this list of what we need to stay spiritually strong is the belt of truth, which we know from previous exploration that Paul tells us to wrap tightly around us—to understand our truth as Christians—our personal truths in God and what we know about our own spiritual strength and beliefs. In other words, our lives must be tightly wrapped in the reality of Jesus Christ. If we are going to win the fight against the enemy, we can't be shuffling between opinions regarding the reality of who Jesus is. We all have to know, inherently, that Jesus is the Son of the living God. Paul tells us to make sure that, as we place that belt of truth around our waists, we also put on the breastplate of righteousness. I like the way that this is translated in the New Century Version of the same clause. The B clause of verse 14 in the New Century Version of the Bible records it this way, "put on the protection of right living in Christ." Isn't that wonderful? The interpretation is simple. As the soldier's breastplate protected his chest from the enemy's attacks, living right guards a believer's heart against the assaults of the devil. We offensively fight the enemy with the word of God, but, here, Paul says that we defensively survive the enemy by living right, set apart unto righteousness, which is when we are living surrendered to God's divine law.

If we are going to win the fight against the enemy, we can't be shuffling between opinions regarding the reality of who Jesus is.

Again, we fight the enemy with the word of God. It's with authority that we have to counter whatever strike the enemy is sending our way. We survive the enemy's blow with the breastplate of righteousness. If we follow the interpretation of the text by staying connected to its original meaning, then it suggests to us that we survive whatever the enemy is doing to hurt, hit, and halt us by living right under the divine law of God. Simply put, we can survive a lot of "stuff "by living right—daily "stuff" like the challenges that work, family, finances, and the world can bring us. We know that we can all get through a lot of stuff when we live right—avoiding a lot of negativity and strife simply by staying on our faithful paths and understanding our faith and our righteousness in God's word. We can, in fact, count on God to show up when we live right. Further, we can depend on God to do certain things for us when He shows up and finds us living right. God will show us new paths, will open new opportunities to us, and will allow us success in this world when…we live absolutely right.

We can depend on God to do certain things for us when He shows up and finds us living right.

Learning to live strong is certainly about how actually learning to fight. Paul is clear about that—fighting, depending on your comfort and confidence with the sword and with the shoes—is important when focused on the right fight. Fighting for what we believe in many ways— by simply standing up to people—talking up the word of the Lord—is what Paul wants us to do. Learning to live strong, Paul intimates, is also about learning how to spiritually survive. Surviving, in general, is about clearly understanding what, within ourselves, needs to be guarded. This is the same with spiritual survival too. Paul says the thing that needs to be guarded most is your heart. He tells us that we don't do that by making our hearts so hard that we don't feel anything when we're hit or damaged. Instead, Paul says that if we love God, we need to maintain a soft heart. The same heart that can be hit and hurt by a person is the same heart that needs to flow love between you, personally, and God. Worship flows from a soft heart, so none of us want our hearts to become so hard that we're unable to feel anything, absorb anything, or extend love to others and God; we do want to maintain a soft and feeling heart—one that is open and loving. What we do to protect it is to put that breastplate over it, so that even when we're hit—when our hearts are targeted—we aren't crushed for good.

The same heart that can be hit and hurt by a person is the same heart that needs to flow love between you, personally, and God.

We all need to surrender to finally seeing right by living under the divine law of God. We need to see living that way as, not only beneficial to developing a healthy relationship between you and God, but living right as a way to provide ourselves and our families the opportunities to live protected. Paul is teaching that living right not only pleases God, but living right also protects all of us, as Christians. Living right not only puts a smile on God's face, but living right puts us in a place to be protected when the enemy gets busy. It is our defense against the enemy's tricks so that whatever the enemy is attempting to do, when we live right, we're covered under a healthy relationship with God and with ourselves.

This all means that you and I can't live believing that there is such a place that is so holy, it is free from attack from the enemies of God. Paul says, "For we wrestle not against flesh and blood but against powers, principalities, and spiritual wickedness in high places." It does not matter how anointed any of us are, we will always, potentially, wrestle against the enemy. The enemy is always doing what the enemy does. The bible says,

"Satan goes to and fro seeking whom he may devour." Many of us believe that we can get anointed enough, holy enough, and the devil will leave us alone. The devil does what the devil does! It is guaranteed that every day that we get up to live our lives the way we always do, if we are disciples of Jesus Christ, the enemy is going to attempt to get us to walk by sight and not by faith, tempting us in many ways as we go about our business.

Many of us believe that we can get anointed enough, holy enough, and the devil will leave us alone.

If we realize that the enemy is always going to try to get us, we can offset these temptations to stray (financially, personally, emotionally, or otherwise) simply by staying on our path of righteousness and protecting ourselves in the ways we've been taught here. Keeping our hearts true and our faith strong may not always feel like enough. Using daily disciplines to reinforce these strengths in our lives will help. Maybe we can spend more time with family, work on ourselves personally by running daily or getting an advanced degree, or maybe we can just make a commitment to give back to our communities—volunteer somewhere or give money to charity. Living a disciplined and happy or fulfilled life is our defense against the enemy. If we find ourselves faced with challenges or doubting our paths, staying faithful, knowing God, and knowing ourselves and what we can accomplish, will help us through it all.

Here is the deeper encouragement we might need: Paul says that, just because the enemy is always on his job, we don't have to walk around full of anxiety. In fact, there is something we can all do that will give us daily confidence to offset attacks on our families, our faith, and our daily lives. In fact, before we leave the house daily, we have to put on the breastplate of righteousness so that when the enemy hits us, it won't destroy us! By doing so, we will bounce back from the hit, stronger and encouraged by our personal strengths, knowing that God has made us stronger than our current, passing stress and stronger than whatever struggle is presenting itself at the moment—because there will be others, but we will be ready.

Before we leave the house daily, we have to put on the breastplate of righteousness so that when the enemy hits us, it won't destroy us!

God has made us all stronger than our sins—no matter how many or how bad we think they are—stronger than our backgrounds no matter how modest or privileged—and stronger than our mistakes because trying and failing only makes us stronger anyway. This is why God has pressed for a supreme place in our lives and done everything possible to get us to choose Him—to choose life over an existence of not living at all. He created a world for all of us that demonstrates, daily, His imaginative grace. And, we should be in awe and inspired daily. Inspiration in daily life is something we should all embrace to allow success and happiness in our lives. We should embrace opportunities for self-examination. When the boss asks us to do a challenging presentation in one evening, for example, we shouldn't complain. We should embrace the opportunity to shine. And, when we have money trouble—a month when the checking account is bottomed out or our bills seem to be too much; we should seek opportunities for new income, actively take a stance on our credit score, and obtaining financial options for ourselves. Or, when God takes a family member or a close friend, we need to take that opportunity to reflect on our relationship with the person, to thank God for our own lives, and to live our futures as fully and as faithfully as we can.

We should embrace the opportunity to shine.

God shaped all of us to live in close relationships with Him. He made us in His image and with a drive to be near Him for all of our lives. Sometimes, when temptations and the "easy way out" come our way, we do stray, but we are meant to be near Him. Like the deer that seeks the brook in the woods, knowing that the nourishment and sustenance of the water will keep him alive, so too the child of God could never be satisfied until the child of God finds him or herself in relationship with a sovereign God—seeking that relationship, satisfied by nothing else.

In many ways, God reminds us of this relationship and how He is taking care of us. God sometimes fulfills our loneliness by shaping somebody similar to us to bring us companionship and help on life's journey whether through marriage or in other friendships and relationships—mentors at work—schoolmates who stay friends for life. If we remain observant, we will see that He sends messages of His will and want and desire for intimate, healthy relationships for you through human vessels and agents: prophets in disguise and priests we encounter in our daily lives, judges and kings with positive influences, apostles and pastors who walk next to us, and teachers and evangelists who remind us of our mission on this earth. They all stand with boldness to correct the misguided thoughts and actions that have the potential to create distance between Him and those He created. God expressed Himself best when He reached into Himself, pulled out Himself and formed and fashioned man and let Jesus be the visible expression of the invisible essence of God. God did all that because He wants to bless you. He doesn't bless you because He feels compelled to do it. God blesses us because He chooses to. The enemy attempts to mess up what God gave us to live in purpose. Living strong is developing a strategy to survive. Paul says the key to surviving is having on the breastplate that protects how you feel about things, because what you are protecting is the heart. Many of us mess up because the enemy does something that hits the heart and the heart responds emotionally in a way that causes dysfunction in the journey. The heart is the emotional center, the source where you wrestle between competitive thoughts and invitations to stray away from what you know is best—and to love and warm to ideas that will help you. In the heart, the deepest and most sincere thoughts you possess exist. If the enemy can catch you without your breastplate on, he aims for the heart and hits you with the intention of getting to you emotionally and, ultimately, getting you to respond to his advances and misguided ideas in the wrong way. Paul reminds us to put on our equipment—our breastplate—our armor—so we can emotionally deal with things the way God intends.

God blesses us because He chooses to.

Remember, our best response when the enemy is getting busy in our lives is to live right. The enemy knows that if we are living right, which means we are spiritually connected, and…if we are spiritually connected, then it won't be long before God will send us all revelation. God will take care of us if we heed what He says.

FOUR:

A STURDY PERSPECTIVE

Ephesians 6:15

 " *…And with your feet fitted with the readiness that comes from the gospel of peace." (NIV)*

NAILED DOWN

Now, as we've established, Paul doesn't miss anything about what this soldier he is chained to is wearing. He knows that everything the soldier is wearing is important for him to faithfully execute his duties as a soldier. Everything is meant for protection or for executing his monumental job when needed. As Paul examines the armor, he knows that each piece is worn or carried to help the soldier stand strong in battle. He has already observed the belt wrapped tightly around the garments of the soldier and equates that with truth. For Paul, it is important that every saint will survive attack by being tightly wrapped in truth, the truth of God, the truth of God's ability to change and convert the human heart, and the truth of God's power to sustain a believer when attacked by the enemy. Paul then sees the breastplate protecting everything from the neck to the navel with particular attention given to the protection of the heart. He equates the breastplate on the soldier with righteousness and righteousness being what protects the Christian heart when the enemy is attacking. He examines the armor as we must examine our own armor in times when truth and righteousness are needed.

As Paul's eyes glance down in further examination, he sees the sandals of the soldier. If it were not for something specific catching his eye, he probably would have passed those sandals by without drawing any spiritual parallel at all. A lot of people wore caligas, which is what such sandals were called, but not everybody had sandals that had a nail driven through them at the toe—like the soldier was wearing. Paul notices this peculiarity regarding the sandals this soldier is wearing. He is quick to note this and to see spiritual parallelisms or the spiritual connection.

Paul knows that the soldier, who has that nail print in his sandals, or perhaps has the actual nail still in, has done some frontline time in battle. Often, while standing on the frontline, a dedicated Roman soldier would submit or volunteer to have his feet nailed to the ground to anchor him in place. When the enemy was advancing, it would be both impossible to run from the chosen spot and the soldier would have to stay and commit to fight—and, it would also make the frontline more impenetrable with soldiers who can't be moved by the enemy, because they are so strongly nailed to the ground.

For Paul, the appropriate theological parallel is easy to draw when he sees this. Just as the soldier is nailed to the ground to secure his place in battle, so he would be harder to move, harder to defeat, and harder to get by—the saint also needs to be secure in battle—nailed to his or her position in the battle with anything that challenges faith. Paul knows immediately what the saint needs in order to hold steady while standing on the frontline in the battle. The saint needs the Gospel of Jesus Christ. For Paul, the Gospel helps you put up the best defense when standing on the frontline of the battle. The Gospel gives you stable and sure footing so you won't be pushed back or allow the enemy to get past you because your footing was shaky or unstable. Paul knows that living strong in the Lord is contingent upon how sure your footing is on the Gospel. You can't expect to survive the attack when you are shaken by what's happening and then shaky about what you are standing on; what it means, its purpose, the limited power your enemy really has in your life, the way God is using it to shape your person.

The Gospel gives you stable and sure footing so you won't be pushed back or allow the enemy to get past you because your footing was shaky or unstable.

How sure is your footing while walking with the Gospel? How much do you really believe that what you read in the Gospel you can manifest in your living? Are you stable enough on the Gospel to use it in quick response to what the enemy is attempting to do in your life or to your life? The Gospel is the extension of God's gracious love which was also to send Jesus; the ministry of Jesus that attached quality of life to what He says is true was the "least of these." His birth, His death, the resurrection, the ascension, His promised return—all of that is the Gospel.

Do you believe and trust the Gospel enough to keep you sure-footed and stable while standing on the frontline in the battle? When your life is under attack do you trust that you are most stable if standing on the

Gospel of Jesus Christ? When the eye of the storm has rested over your life, do you believe that the Gospel is still your best solution so that when the storm passes over you will be found standing on the frontline, strong because you stood on the Gospel? Paul says that if you want to live strong in the Lord's mighty power when Satan is advancing with tricks and schemes, then you have to prepare by binding your feet to the Gospel of peace. Paul is not suggesting this is something God is going to do by way of miracle. Paul says YOU have to do it. You have to believe that the Gospel is the sturdiest place upon which you can stand especially when the enemy is attacking you. You have to prepare yourself by putting the Gospel under your stand. When the enemy is attacking, the questions we must all answer include: Is the life and the ministry of Jesus enough to encourage you, sustain you, empower you, inform you, and motivate you? Paul says the Gospel ought to produce peace for every saint. You ought to be able to stand right in the middle of satanic attack and find inspiration in the Gospel of Jesus. In the face of life's toughest decisions, you ought to be able to draw strength and confidence from the life and ministry of Jesus and the message His life portrays. The essence of the message of the Gospel is that the rejected can be accepted make a difference. When you have deep spirituality, you are approachable and can be counted on to manifest compassion, forgiveness, and love. The message of the Gospel says: With God, everything is possible.

When your life is under attack do you trust that you are most stable if standing on the Gospel of Jesus Christ?

Paul knows everybody loves and affirms the Gospel before the battle. In fact, we all feel that we know the Gospel from attending church on Sunday, and we feel strong most of the time in defending our faith. As we've learned in previous chapters, however, sometimes we are attacked and we don't realize it! We are swayed by others, weakened by adversity in life—and we are no longer nailed to our position. We can learn from Paul, who says that if you stand your life on the Gospel expecting it to give you peace, you don't just shout it, you don't just profess it, you demonstrate it. You demonstrate it by being willing to be nailed to the ground on the frontline in the battle when all you have to fight with is the Gospel.

The challenge that comes to us is that, often, the Gospel will challenge us beyond cognitive acceptance, beyond whether you believe what was said to have been a part of the life of Jesus. The Gospel challenges us beyond emotional absorption. Its primary aim is to get you to do something in response to having surrendered to being transformed. You have to give in to what is expected of you completely in order to be transformed in the Lord—in order to get to that impenetrable line of defense. Many times, we are asked to do things that are not comfortable but are the right things to do. We may feel the pain of giving up certain luxuries—certain habits—only to prove our faith and our fortitude in faith and with God.

You have to give in to what is expected of you completely in order to be transformed in the Lord—in order to get to that impenetrable line of defense.

The essence of measuring someone's transformation occurs by watching his or her actions. Everything Jesus taught and said invited people not to just accept what He said as truth, but to go out and do it. And, back then, what He was saying and what He was rebelling against would have been hard, at times, to get behind. It required bravery and sacrifice, and only a few were up to the task. And, to this day, we all know that the hard reality could be that the Lord allows certain attacks, situations, and challenges in our lives. We may not always see them coming or know what to think about them, but if your faith—your armor—your belt of truth—your position nailed in place—are all part of your daily approach to God and to faith, you will persevere and succeed.

Maybe a lot of what God is allowing is the result of us not changing what we do in response to what He expects or what He wants us to challenge ourselves with. Maybe, when we are called to action—to charity—to ministry—to the simple support of others—we should heed that call—become proactive self-starters in our faith and remain ready to intercept and beat adversity or challenges to our faith and the foundation and faith of others. Remember, what Paul sees about this soldier's sandals are what makes him different and unique as a soldier, perhaps from other soldiers. He was willing to be nailed to the frontline for what he was defending and willing to put his life on the line for what he believed. Others didn't do this, and Paul sees this nail and knows at some point that the soldier has been forced by choice or circumstances to stand on the frontline. He understands his fortitude—and he sees that his stance or his experience is stronger than others; again, either because he's been thrown into adversity or chosen to address certain challenges, this all makes him more formidable and better for his experiences.

We can see, like Paul, that his soldier has been challenged by battle, and that he is not some novice or "rookie" guard, because they would not have assigned a rookie guard to watch an important public perceived criminal like the apostle Paul. And, as Paul mulls this over, he realizes that his faith may match the battle fortitude of this soldier. And, every day, we all need to assume that we need to be stronger than the challenges that will await us. We need to be as formidable as we can be so than what may rock our faith or take us off our path to success in all that we seek to destroy or offset.

We all need to assume that we need to be stronger than the challenges that will await us.

The soldier in this story has been around; he's done his time, but he's also been a demonstrator. Some battle has taken place, and the bible does tell us that every one of the seed of David will spend their lives fighting. Since all of us are of the seed of David, there is no place in God where you can be so anointed that you will live above a battle. At some point in all our lives, we will be called to fight in some way. Every day that we all get up, we are putting on armor to go out to engage a battle. What Paul is challenging us to accept is that, while profession and confession are good, there has to be, in the body, some incarnation followed by some demonstration. In other words, we need to know what needs to be done, be ready for it, and then…execute it—demonstrate our faith, our strength, our fortitude in being nailed to our battleground.

Every day that we all get up, we are putting on armor to go out to engage a battle.

The Gospel is calling you to—not just affirm its reality—but to live out what it says. You take the Gospel to your battlefield, and if you really trust the word, don't throw it out there for chance; instead, nail yourself to the frontline and be willing to take the hit. And, you can take the hit, because you know that you believe. Nail yourself down to this path—to this battle—so that you won't have any flexibility to run or retreat when the battle gets thick. Don't leave yourself with any other options but the Gospel. If you believe the Gospel to be the power of God, nail yourself there on the battlefield and demonstrate how willing you are to fight. If you lose the battle, then the Gospel isn't real, but if you win the battle, then you can't credit anything but the Gospel. And, I assure you, if you do nail yourself to the battlefield, you will win—your faith will prevail. Again, these battles may randomly come to us during the day. Issues in life will challenge our faith—people will try to lead us astray. If we plan to demonstrate our faith and live by it, then we need to be ready for anything and open to our own empowerment—in order to keep that faith strong.

German-born, Lutheran pastor and theologian, Dietrich Bonheoffer, was part of a small, rebellious dissident group who together attempted to assassinate Adolph Hitler. He was a preacher when he joined the group, which thought the best thing they could do for the advancement of the kingdom was to assassinate the crazed Adolph Hitler. Bonheoffer was so committed that he nailed his convictions metaphorically to the frontline of the battle against Nazism and was arrested. He was arrested still writing about Jesus, arrested still preaching about Jesus, and arrested still standing on the secure foundation of Jesus. He was executed and hanged because he believed in Jesus. He was hung up, because he was nailed down. His faith remained strong, however, and he did not die in vein—because his actions and the movement he helped set in motion eventually did work to involve other like-minded people and bring down the evil Nazi regime.

Martin Luther King, Jr. was shot on the balcony of the Lorraine Motel in Memphis, because he was nailed down on the frontline. He believed that if you know Jesus then you have got to fight social injustice and stand on the frontline against cultural oppression. If you know Jesus then you've got to preach that all men have come out of one blood. He stood by his convictions every day and was happy and strong in his fight to make this a better world. In this way, he lived a fulfilled and faithful life with no regrets, he changed the world, and he stayed true to the Gospel— what he got from the Word of God.

If you know Jesus then you've got to preach that all men have come out of one blood.

In this story, Paul, nailed to the ground—in prison and facing execution, told his young understudy, Timothy, not to cry over what was about to happen to him. He was ready to be offered up; he fought a good fight, and he kept the faith.

And, of course, we can't forget that Jesus was nailed to a cross, because He was nailed on the frontline of His own convictions. Because, Jesus believed the Word to do what the Word said it would do, He nailed Himself to it. If you are going to live strong and fight mighty, you will have to nail yourself down on the Gospel of Jesus Christ.

SECOND INSTALLMENT:

A TESTIMONIAL TO THE ARMOR OF GOD

Friends are valued components in a well-lived life. It might sound odd to word it that way, but, truly, they are these necessary cogs in the daily grind of life. They are more than confidants and people to pal around with; they truly shape a large part of our worlds. They are people we talk to when we are down—and they provide comfort in the face of family, professional, or other issues. They share large components of our lives, often the people who knew us when we were small children or in college or just starting our careers and families. They are important!

In the last few years, I've observed a couple of unfortunate instances with friendships dissolving or experiencing trouble—either because of a miscommunication or another equally as trite issue. Sometimes, the issues are valid and get blown out of proportion, and other times, the issues are clouded by our own insecurities or issues that we or those close to us project onto others.

In one case, I knew of two women, who, for as long as I knew them, had been in the same social circles. I did not know them to mix or connect on their own, but they were at all church events together, shared a number of friends, and interacted without incident all the time. One day, another woman from the same circle of friends came to me and told me that they were not speaking and that one of them refused to be in the same room with the other. The other woman simply ignored her aggressor's silent treatment and requests to stay away. As a result, the more vocal of the two began to retreat and not to interact with anyone at all, simply to avoid this other woman. The other woman, while trying to ignore it all, was a sensitive sort and was experiencing health and sleep issues due to the stress of this other woman and her wild claims. This third party wanted to know how to help them and to help those who had to put up with the awkward silences and hostile behavior. It was affecting the whole group of friends in this church and community.

Apparently, the one woman—we'll call her Jane—had wanted the other woman to change the date of a party she had planned. When the other woman—we'll call her Sara—refused, Jane planned a dinner outing with friends and excluded her. When Sara called to ask why she had been excluded and raised her voice to Jane a bit, Jane began telling her how she never liked her or her children—felt she was a spoiled phony— did not care for her attitude—did not appreciate being "re-gifted" for her birthday and more. When Sara tried to respond, Jane hung up. For me, just learning the dynamic of the event that set it all off helped me to understand the dilemma a bit. It seemed to me that Jane had long harbored some resentments toward Sara but had never opened up to her about her concerns, and it appeared that Sara had always, perhaps, not noticed Jane at all or had not regarded her as a friend—ever. Again, it seemed that they had never approached these issues or talked them out.

For me, it seemed that they were both suffering and that a solution was just around the corner. The third party told me, however, that Jane was adamant about excluding Sara and that she often spoke harshly of her—calling her stupid or trashy. Sara, on the other hand, had, apparently, always reached out to Jane. The "re-gifting" incident was actually because she had gone out of her way to find a wine and a special lunch bag for Jane for her birthday. She knew that Jane was picky and that, as a teacher, she liked to take her lunch to school. She got her the same wine she saw at Jane's house for a Christmas party—and she ordered a flowered bag that Jane had admired. Jane accused her of stealing the bottle of wine and giving it to her as a gift—and also giving her a bag that she knew she already had so that she would just return it and not have to pay. Of course, she only said all this behind Sara's back and never asked her about it. And, further, as "punishment" for her "re-gifting," Jane had taken a gift intended for Sara's teenage daughter at a holiday gift exchange and would not give it back. Sara ignored the incident and so did everyone else. According to the third party, everyone had known for a while that Jane had "problems."

Because Jane had been in the church longer, she had a larger group of acquaintances and was getting quite good at excluding Sara. Sara was from a family that had a little bit of money, and she was a big personality—gregarious, friendly, stylish, and fun. My third party contact for this situation informed me that, long before the "re-gifting" incident, Jane would say to Sara's face, "You have an advanced degree? Well, you don't seem like someone who even went to school."—Or—"Please don't hold my baby; you seem a little odd to me." Sara would tear up on occasion or get embarrassed but would never say anything, mostly because, according to the third party observer, everyone was a little afraid of Jane—knew they would suffer her wrath or even push her away when she clearly had problems and needed people around her. Sara, as the gentle one in the situation, was being made to suffer.

Soon after counseling this third party observer, I found out that Sara had recently lost her father and two college friends to cancer—all within a short time. I discovered that Jane was telling people it was because she was a bad person—that she had no sympathy for her—and, further, was using Sara's grief to continue to exclude her from events and outings, saying that Sara didn't want to go or would ruin it with her demeanor. Jane was using Sara's absence to gather people to her "side," telling them that Sara had screamed at her the day of the initial "argument" and threatened her and that she would not include her until she got an apology from her—in front of the whole group. None of this was true, of course, and, although it was probably Sara who was owed and apology and support, no one was going to step forward and tell the truth or remedy the situation, because they were all afraid of Jane. It became clear to me that both women needed counseling and that I would have to intervene.

I did not feel it was my place to approach each woman, so I, first, counseled the group of female friends surrounding the two women. I reminded them of their commitment to a firm stance in faith—a commitment to wearing truth proudly and using it as a defense—a commitment to being a Christian and all that entailed, including being righteous and living strong in God—living strong in the face of something that is wrong—living strong in the face of a fellow Christian who needed help and another who needed guidance to get off the wrong path. I reminded them how evil in any form—jealousy and rage—could cause even the most faithful to stray and to affect others. I told them that they all knew what they needed to do. They needed to confront Jane and right her on the path to Jesus and her commitment to Christian love and inclusion. And, they also needed to minister to Sara and let her know that, even though they didn't know her as well, they were there for her and would not put up with exclusion and dishonesty. They had to stand firm in faith and use their Armor of God to resist the negative influences and to help both people in need—all judgment, anger, and fear aside.

The women did what I told them. They elected the two most faithful and strong in the group to approach each woman. Sara was grateful and reduced to tears. She agreed that some anger had built up over time and she wanted to talk to me about that, as her pastor. Jane remained hostile. She stormed out of the meeting and has since refused to interact with the group. Slowly, she is singling people out for counsel, though it is unclear whether or not she is thinking positively or negatively. It is clear to most who interact with her, however, that she is making unconscious "baby steps" as a result of the intervention of faith to make herself more well-rounded, focus on her own family and hobbies, and develop herself a bit. All, hopefully, taking her down the path to being less insecure and more solid with God and relationships with others. I am proud of the group, however, because they continue to stay the path and include Sara while reaching out to Jane—faith, truth, righteousness, Armor of God and all firmly in place.

FIVE:

USING THE SHIELD OF FAITH

Ephesians 6:16

"In addition to all this, take up the shield of faith with which you can extinguish all the flaming arrows of the evil one." (NIV)

One additional translation records verse 16 this way:

"In every battle you will need faith as your shield to stop the fiery arrows armed at you by Satan." (TLB)

Another one says:

"At all times carry faith as a shield; for with it you will be able to put out all the burning arrows shot by the Evil One." (GNT)

WHAT IS OUR "SHIELD OF FAITH"?

Paul is chained to this Roman soldier, assigned to basically guard this religious threat. Paul has learned to seek God in everything—but experience as design, as we've established thus far in the book. For us, in examination of this text, he is using the armor of the soldier to teach the proper spiritual dress for one who is determined to live strong in the Lord's mighty power. For Paul in his physical situation, he notices the inconvenient, weighty shield in the hand of the soldier, which is comprised of two huge pieces of wood that are glued together and held awkwardly in the guard's hand. The shield is four feet high and two and a half feet wide—it is huge in comparison to his body.

In noticing all that, Paul becomes struck by the importance of that shield to that soldier. The belt, the breastplate, and the nailed sandals are only effective if they can all be protected by this formidable shield, which the soldier holds in his hands. Further, if we notice in our examination of this text, Paul places particular emphasis on this shield and draws our attention to the serious nature of what he is about to teach us. Whatever translation you prefer, verse 16 starts something like this, "Above all else." One translation has it, "Over all these." Still another says, "In addition to all of these, take the shield of faith." That placement of those words, "in addition," "above all," "over all," is very interesting because, in all those translations, Paul puts this huge shield before the helmet of salvation. He also puts it before the sword of the spirit, but, strategically places it after the belt, the breastplate, and the shoes, which is interesting in the implication for what it means to us as Christians, fighting the good fight every day. What should we put first? What should we place most emphasis on? Where should we concentrate our energy? And, finally, does it help if we know in which order we should be handling all of our defenses against the forces that oppose us and our faith?

While we will point to why the other two elements—the helmet and the sword—were not included in this "above all" suggestion when it comes to taking the shield of faith, the important lesson is the need to protect the truth or the belt—the need to protect the heart or the breastplate—and the need to protect the determination to stand fighting on the firm foundation of the good news of Jesus or the shoes with the nails, ready for battle, and ready for the gospel of peace. Paul is attempting to intimate that all of these need to be protected by the shield of faith. Faith in this verse means to have resolute belief in God—fixed, firm, determined belief in God. Paul says our faith becomes a shield for us. We need that because the enemy is always releasing fiery darts. He's always releasing flaming arrows. And, it is important to note, here, that the shield DOES have to protect the breastplate and the lifeblood of the heart, the vulnerable belt of truth, and the often unwilling or scared firm plant of the shoes of faith on the ground. These are tricky, vulnerable, and challenging areas. The helmet of salvation is a gift to us—something we are given and wear proudly; it doesn't require the same cumbersome, but necessarily sturdy, shield of faith. It certainly goes hand in hand with the shield of faith—is worn just as proudly—but requires less work and not as much attention. Whereas, the heavy and often hard to manage shield of faith requires strength to use and maintain.

Paul says our faith becomes a shield for us.

Back to our text, the Roman soldier understood that his enemy would often dip his arrow in pitch and then set it ablaze so that when it penetrated the intended target, the object or person would be engulfed in flames, if not killed by the arrow itself. The destruction would come twofold—from the piercing of the arrow itself, and, from the foolproof strike of the fire. This shield could protect against both, and Paul quickly understood the spiritual connection. And, as Christians, managing our own shields of faith now—and our own defenses against the enemy now—we must understand it too.

The enemy is also often releasing arrows. He dips them in lies, tricks, and schemes. If he can't kill you with the strike of what he releases, he hopes to inflame something that will consume you until you are no longer effective and perhaps totally destroyed. Flaming arrows are words that may define you improperly or offend you, but they also penetrate enough that you add them, albeit unintentionally in some cases, to your meditations and feelings about who you are, what you want out of life, and who will be significant to and in your life. Flaming arrows are seeds planted in you by others under demonic influence until you start living to prove them right or prove them wrong, rather than living to be obedient to God. Flaming arrows are circumstances intended to make you doubt your confidence and regret your steps, and second-guess your decisions. What's important for you to get is that Paul is saying to you that they are just that—fiery darts—flaming arrows—easy to deflect with your sturdy shield of faith.

Flaming arrows are circumstances intended to make you doubt your confidence and regret your steps, and second-guess your decisions.

Now, granted, many have been taken out by the darts, pierced in vital places of the mind and the heart and of the emotions until the strike itself just took them out—made them insecure or unhappy—sent them down the wrong paths in life—or allowed them to reject people and goals important to them. Others have absorbed the darts but have been taken out by the fire, because they keep that shield close—they lessen the impact with their faith and all that it protects and holds close—their sense of truth—their stability in the fight against the enemy—and their spirituality and heart. However, for some, the fiery dart is so damaging because while the faithful may survive the hit, he or she may not be able to put out the flame. And, again, we all know these feelings that creep in—I can't finish school—I can't be in the marriage—I'm not capable of this job—I don't like church anymore. These are inflamed and very damaging thoughts that plague any of us who give in years from now, and, over time, make us doubt our strengths, and gifts, and purpose, and power. At the time, we know it in our hearts that we should not listen, but the flames are powerful and fast-moving. If we are not expecting the fire, then we will have trouble in our defenses against it.

Again, these are all inflamed suggestions that can make the best of us build decisions based on over-exaggerated data, or decisions on high-octane emotions without sufficient theological rebuttals and too little faith and trust in God. As I said before, we have all been hit by them, haven't we? We know their power; we know what it's like to let these feelings and urges get the better of us. What's more important is that Paul says, based on verse 16, that we all have a response to this. We have a response when flaming arrows have been released and aimed in our direction. Our response is always to take up our shields, those often heavy but very protective symbol of faith against anything. Our motivation for doing this is that we have already wrapped ourselves in truth that we're not willing to give up so easily. We are attempting to live under God's divine order, and we want to stay focused on that. We all want to trust our truths, stand in order even in a battle. Because of that, we are willing to be nailed down on whom we all know as God is and what we know God can do—no matter what others say or do. Even though we know the enemy is a good archer, what protects us when we are trying to grow, trying to honor God—what protects us from going back, slipping giving up, from relinquishing power—and what protects us is taking up the shield of faith. Paul says that shield deflects arrows, and it protects the other pieces of the armor as well—all those other components of truth, love, and strength that we've put in place.

We are attempting to live under God's divine order, and we want to stay focused on that.

Our faith does a couple of things. Number one, our faith intercepts fiery darts. Every day that soldier puts on pieces of the armor. Not one piece he puts on can stop an arrow from penetrating except the shield and the helmet—that faith that he holds and maintains—and that helmet given to him to keep him safe. He knows that if an attack comes, his skills are honed. They are developed to fight what is in front of him. He is trained and prepared for that. He has already felt that kind of engagement, but the soldier can't always stop what will be released in the air aimed in his direction. He can't stop all the arrows that will be released coming in his direction, so he takes the shield and he carries it. He knows that, at the end of the day, what will have saved his life is that shield. It might have arrows sticking out of it, but it is better that arrows are sticking out of it than arrows sticking out of him. He knows, at the end of the day, when he sits down and wipes sweat from his brow and decides to take sustenance to strengthen him for the battle of tomorrow, he's pulling arrows out of his shield that would have done major damage. He may even have burned entry places on that wooden shield where flying, fiery darts, dipped in pitch have hit his shield, but he'll be carrying it, having intercepted the arrows. Our faith will take a beating in a given day, but with that shield to protect all that we put in place—all that we know is us—we are protected, and we maintain who we are and where we want to go.

When the soldier rests for the evening, part of his evening prayer of intimate gratitude to God is that he is pulling out of the shield the arrows sent and aimed in his direction, intended to take him out. Now he is tossing away what was intended to take him out. Paul says that, like that soldier, everyday ewe must rise and remind ourselves of the truth of who God is. We need to wrap this truth tightly around our waists—the truth of who God created us to be, the truth about what God wants to accomplish in our lives—wrap it all tightly like a belt around your tunic. Every day, submit yourself to the fight! We all know we are going to the battlefield, so we can't go to the battlefield hoping that we won't have to fight. We must go to the battlefield already resolute that if we're on the battlefield and a fight is going to ensue, we may as well fight—and win.

We need to wrap this truth tightly around our waists— the truth of who God created us to be.

79

We need to fight every day to submit ourselves to live under God's divine order, on the Lord's side, excited to defend the causes of the kingdom of the sovereign God, ready to advance His will. We must nail ourselves down on the power of Jesus' person. We must nail ourselves down on the power of Jesus' name. We must nail ourselves down on the power of Jesus' promises. Let these secure us in place—indefinitely. If we have to stand on the frontline, and when the battle starts, we fight. We must fight the good fight of faith. It's easy to fight when we can clearly see the enemy in front of you. However, beware, because in the spiritual realm, Satan is going to be releasing fiery darts, flaming arrows, things we can't always see coming or even anticipate. We can't stop Satan from releasing and aiming these flaming arrows at us, but we can intercept them if we have resolute, fixed, firm, determined beliefs in a sovereign God.

We can't stop everything released and aimed at us, but we can stop letting everything released at us have access. We can't stop what Satan does, but we don't have to let it penetrate our thinking, our emotions, our actions, and our responses. We need the shield of faith—consistently. The arrows or the enemy will strike, but nothing should draw blood. We may come in dragging a shield full of arrows, but we ought not to come in with puncture wounds from what people have said or what situations have created for us in the way of challenges and tragedies. We have to believe in God until we're so resolute that even released arrows aimed at us have to stop at the place of our beliefs—especially when our beliefs are so strong that they nearly attack the enemy in defense.

We can't stop what Satan does, but we don't have to let it penetrate our thinking, our emotions, our actions, and our responses.

How deep are arrows able to penetrate in your life? How much damage can a flaming arrow do before you address it? Why are you pulling arrows out of you rather than your shield? Paul says you have to be able to intercept these arrows with your faith until you know that what you heard is someone's opinion based on their own set of data and experiences. You can't do anything about arrows being released, but you can do something about where they lodge. Not only does your faith intercept fiery darts and flaming arrows, Paul says your faith extinguishes them. Your faith, one translation says, has the ability to "quench the fiery darts of the evil one."

To further the analogy for our own lives, remember—that soldier puts his armor on, picks up his shield, and on the front of that shield are bands of leather overlaying the outer portion of that shield. The soldier anticipates that one of the most effective weapons of the adversary is the arrow aimed from far away, because sometimes the enemy is too cowardly to fight you up close. Many times, the enemy releases arrows in large numbers, a consistent barrage of released arrows because he's hoping that while all of them may not strike, one may be fatal. That soldier has learned that when the enemy is trying to do damage they will place on fire the tipped end of the arrow before they release it. The soldier takes extra time each day to wet the leather and the wood on the shield. Wet wood is heavier wood, but he would rather carry the heavier shield if it can quench a fiery dart. The reason he does this is because he knows that he may have to walk in the dry desert with flaming arrows coming to dry wood unless he wets it down. He also does it because if his shield becomes enflamed, not only does he put his own life in jeopardy, but he puts the lives of the soldiers on the side fighting with him in jeopardy as well. So, every day, he grabs his shield and dips it in water to make sure it is wet down for the whole day. He prepares—he offsets the enemy with his defense, nurturing and taking care of what will, ultimately, take care of him.

There are times when we can't take a dry faith to a fresh battle, and we have to remember that.

Paul says, like the soldier, our shields of faith not only intercept arrows but they will extinguish the thirst of any flaming arrows coming our way. Our shields do this when we present to our battles shields that have been saturated in active faith—nurtured, cared for, and prepped for what is awaiting us in opposition. The soldier is implying to us that there are some battles where you cannot take a dry shield and expect to win a fresh battle. There are times when we can't take a dry faith to a fresh battle, and we have to remember that. We have to wet it down with a fresh encounter with a holy God, with fresh engagement from a holy word, with fresh fellowship among a holy people, and giving God fresh worship in a holy place. We need for God to wet our faith with fresh revelation, and, suddenly, inspiration and the promise of right provide protection, because we can't make it in some battles on a historical experience, and we know what it takes in our daily lives. We all need to know that God has already said that, right now—at any given time, He is going to get us through what we are facing or will inevitably face. Every day, we have to dip our shields in fresh revelation, because the enemy is coming with fresh weapons.

So, in summary, that shield intercepts, that shield extinguishes, but that shield is heavy, particularly when you, faithful readers, are trying to carry it all of the time. It is not easy to carry that shield everywhere you go. While you appreciate it when you need it, it can sometimes feel like a weight when you don't think you need it. If we're honest, faith can be a heavy weight sometimes. Faith sometimes can be heavy on the journey, because that shield makes us think about some things we don't want to consider. It is a reminder that we are carrying a responsibility that we can't do everything we want to do or say everything we want to say. We have to be faithful to fighting the way God instructs us to fight. You don't carry the heavy load of faith because it is easy. You carry the heavy load of faith because it is effective. Don't give up on faith!

> ### *Faith sometimes can be heavy on the journey, because that shield makes us think about some things we don't want to consider.*

Recently, I became aware of a pastor who lost his eleven-year-old son to an instant illness, and I know he struggled with why God would let that happen. This was particularly hard—even for those not close to the situation—because not long after burying his oldest son for another reason, his youngest son became stricken with a fatal disease and died.

A few weeks after burying him, the pastor himself was diagnosed with prostate cancer. After preaching a powerful message on faith, his parishioners went to him and asked, "How do you keep preaching faith when God has allowed all of these atrocities to befall you?" He backed up, squared his shoulders and said, "I really did want to give up, but one day I took my bible and I went in the sanctuary. I sat in the pew and cracked open my bible and it happened to fall on the psalms. I fell on a passage where the psalmist said, 'the Lord is good'. Then my exegetical mind kicked into gear, because I noticed when I read that the psalmist didn't put any qualifiers on his expression 'the Lord is good.' The psalmist just merely said the Lord is good, period." There are things we won't understand—and there are challenges that seem beyond us right now—but we are capable and God is still God. Life is good, but life is full of challenges and the unexpected. There is no guarantee that it will always be easy. God is there no matter what. He doesn't allow things to happen; He, instead, provides us with opportunities for strength and faith that get us through it all.

Part of what gives you intimacy with God, dear readers, is every time you see all the charred puncture holes in those shields, you know that they are symbols of survival. You have been through some stuff that your faith was able to intercept and extinguish. Although it is heavy to carry at times, it is worth it. It's better to be fatigued in faith than destroyed and devoid of God in your lives.

SIX:

USING THE HELMET OF SALVATION

Ephesians 6:17

"Take the helmet of salvation and the sword of the Spirit, which is the word of God." (NIV)

HELMET OF SALVATION

The attack Satan launches on the life of a believer certainly has as an intention to penetrate wherever he finds a spiritual opening. The goal is to get believers to denounce our faith, to surrender our hope in God, or to accept as a truth what is really a lie. Generalized, we could say Satan attacks our belief systems. He attacks the weakness or fragility of what we believe to be truth in our lives. The goal is to get us to drop a loosely wrapped belt of truth for a lie or a manipulated truth until our movement and agility are negatively affected. Satan attacks truth in our lives because, when he attacks the truth, it can severely impair our positive progress.

Paul says to us that when we want to make sure we are protected with truth, every day, when we get up, we must tightly wrap the belt of truth around us—surround ourselves with what we know to be true—fill our minds with it. Satan also wants to attack our standards. If Satan can find but a mere opening in our lives where, perhaps, there is a lack of commitment to living under the direct Divine Order of God, he will settle for attacking that. Keep in mind, he is trying to see if you believe living under God's Divine Order is only an option among many options for, or if it is a conviction that stands alone and will stand up to anything. Paul says you counter-attack this when, every day, from the neck to the navel, you are covered with the breastplate of righteousness. Satan will also settle for attacking where you've drawn your lines and where you've decided to anchor yourself, and, further, with which you nail your life down. When he finds that you are not nailed down on a fixed, determined, and resolute belief in God, Satan knows it won't be hard to push you off of the frontline of your own core values and convictions. We are all vulnerable to this and, therefore, Paul says we all must counter that when our shoes are readied with the Gospel of Peace and when the truth surrounds us.

Satan also wants to attack our standards.

Satan will also settle for concentrating on your fixed belief in God, the things you say are absolutes about your relationship to God. He fights that in the way that he does, not because he thinks he can destroy your faith but because he is convinced he can get you to drop your faith. He keeps a constant barrage of flaming arrows and fiery darts aimed and released in your direction—all to shake up your defenses and your beliefs. We know that Paul says you counter all of that by taking up the shield of faith.

Paul has disciplined himself, while chained to this Roman guard, to draw these spiritual parallels between the armor of the soldier and the metaphorical dress necessary for a believer to stay true to his or her path. Paul sees on the soldier the bronze helmet worn to protect the most vital area—his head. Ultimately, too, this helmet would protect his mind, and, in turn, his very life—spiritual for us believers—his actual life for the soldier—both very important. In all of these areas Satan will settle for as an opening, an entry into our lives—spiritual or otherwise. Readers—be aware that Satan's prime target of attack is to get into the control center of your mind. It is the control center of your mind—the conscious center of analytical thought—that first accepts the possibility of faith. It is the control center of the mind that responds to the invitation of faith. It is the control center of the mind that finally submits to a life of faith. It is the mind that believes God is God. This must be protected.

Be aware that Satan's prime target of attack is to get into the control center of your mind.

Finally, once the mind is satisfied, then it is the heart that follows, which is why we are encouraged to be transformed by the renewing of our mind first in our faith—then our hearts. To review—salvation is not about getting a new heart, but it is about getting a changed mind. Living in faith is not about getting a new heart, but it is about getting a transformed mind. What you will discover about your own life is that much of what you think needs to change is not necessarily about the items for change as much as it is about your mind concerning everything needing to change. The mind forms strategies and communicates with every other part of who you are. Whatever the mind ponders, the mind can order produced. Satan attacks the mind by attempting to do one thing above everything else: to tempt you to despair about your life. That means to lose hope or to lose confidence in God's abilities, in your survival, and, ultimately, to lose hope and confidence in your very existence. Once you believe that there is no way to pull out of a situation, and once you believe that there is no way for a situation to turn around—and, finally, once you believe that there is no positive to a negative, Satan knows you will stop fighting to win. You will start making unnecessary mistakes in judgment and action, because you'll wake up every day just trying not to lose. You will be on guard instead of confident in your path.

Satan attacks the mind by attempting to do one thing above everything else: to tempt you to despair about your life.

While we Christians don't often talk about it and while it is not preached enough, despair grips us in large numbers and with a tight hold. Readers—I've been in ministry for over two decades now, and I will confess to you that I've never before in ministry encountered the kind of despair that is pervasive in the current church culture. There are Christians suffering from despair, which is, as we know, a feeling of utter hopelessness or living with a "give up" attitude. They wake up every day with the expectation that the sky is falling, that the world is crumbling, that life is useless, and that people are evil at the core. It is what one writer calls "de-motivators," which suggests that despair is the eruption and landslide of de-motivators. We all know that de-motivators are full of mistakes, regrets, failures, conditions, circumstances, and disappointments. And, that it is in dwelling on such things that we, ultimately, fail. Certainly, we are allowed mistakes. It is what we do with them and with what we've learned that more clearly defines us. Unfortunately, many times, we Christians allow the enemy to attack the control center of the mind until we drown in a sea of demotivating thoughts and demotivating circumstances. Once that happens, it totally deadens energy, it robs enthusiasm, and it strips us of positive self-affirmations. These are all necessary to a well-lived, confident, truthful, and Christian life of faith.

We all know that de-motivators are full of mistakes, regrets, failures, conditions, circumstances, and disappointments.

Once this happens to any of us, we risk becoming no fun to be around at all. Beyond that, we risk becoming a literal drag to everyone we talk to or encounter, thereby risking their fall into despair as well. As one who has fallen victim to this, you're talking, but you're dragging everyone down with what you're saying. The problem is, over the course of time, you know it—you realize what is happening, and it can become worse. I've seen it happen many times. Faithful people will let time pass and will begin to distance themselves from the mainstream and start to slide into a darkened existence, what educator, community leader, and theologian, Howard Thurman, refers to as the "dark night of the soul." The pain is hard to pinpoint, and many times, people often wonder why they feel down and are living and talking so negatively. As intelligent people, it is easy to figure, reasonably, that some things contribute to the feeling, but it is often hard to say what it really is. To those experiencing it, it is just despair. This is so different than our Christian forbearers who, despite spiritual persecution, religious infancy, and just a few years removed from Jesus' crucifixion, had a different response to the attack of despair. 20th Century Methodist Christian missionary and theologian, E. Stanley Jones, in his book Abundant Living, says that "the early Christians never said in dismay, 'look at what the world has come to' but in delight the early Christians said, 'look at what has come to the world. Jesus.' They saw not merely the ruin but the resource for the reconstruction of the ruin. They saw not merely that sin that abound but they celebrated that where sin did abound grace did much more abound. On that assurance the pivot of history swung from blank despair, loss of moral nerve and fatalism to faith and confidence that at last in Jesus, sin had met its match."

In this latest analysis in the book, we find that Paul gives us the piece of armor that we need to use to respond to the enemy's attempt to get into the control center of the mind—our reasonable, analytical mind from which all beliefs and lifestyle decisions are stored—and bring about the explosive nature of mental despair. We, too, can see God's hand at work even in our darkest moments. We, too, can see God's will prevailing through our toughest trials. We too, instead of seeing the negative that makes us want to stop fighting, ought to see the positive that makes us believe that God is too good for us to quit, God is too good for us to stop fighting, and God is too good for us to give up. He's good no matter what.

Paul says that, in order to get there, we all need to take the helmet of salvation—the protector of the mind and what all that entails—our spiritual life and beyond. Here, unlike verses 13 and 16 that talk about "taking" as well, "take" here is not that you can by your own control, power, or authority **take** the helmet of salvation. In this text, it is not referring to "take" in the traditional sense of the word. You don't **take** salvation; you **receive** salvation. This is critical to understand and implement, because many of us have so meshed secular humanism into our attempt to have authentic spirituality, and we bring so much of US into our spirituality, that God has been lowered and diluted down to an equivalent friend, a peer—as if we can go to God and snatch from him what we want. You don't take salvation. You have to wait for salvation to be extended. When you confess to Jesus and repent of sin, God extends salvation.

The helmet of salvation protects this critical place of attack, the control center of the mind. Paul is not just talking about salvation as mere conversion and is he not talking about salvation merely as eternal destination. All of us have been saved from the penalty of sin. All of us are saved unto eternity with God. All of us also need to be saved from the power of sin. I'm grateful that I have been converted. I'm grateful that there is a reserved spot for me in eternity, but I'm also grateful that God is doing some stuff within me in between all the salvation that I know.

All of us also need to be saved from the power of sin.

Salvation is the Greek word "soterian," meaning I surrender my life to Jesus. Paul says this helmet of salvation, this placing on the mind a surrender—a "soterian"—is key to our lives. This helmet or protection suggests to all of us that we have anchored a hope in our relationships with Jesus that is most powerful when we're under attack. In fact, under any attack, we can have a hope that the God who has saved us—and the God who has reserved a place for us in eternity—is the God whose salvation does something about us under attack in our current lives. It is my hope; it should be your hope, readers. This premise suggests that what differentiates us from people in the world when living under attack is that we don't have to have a mindset of fatalism, because we always live with the hope that God has saved, God will reserve, but God is going to do something about what we're going through right now—individuals, communities, and the world. As Christians, our hope has been anchored in that man who died on that center cross and got up from a borrowed tomb, who we believe is alive, seated at the right hand of the Father and is coming back to rapture His church for an eternity in God's presence. We live according to the Scriptures, because it is the manual that feeds our hope. We respond to live in certain ways, because we believe God to be the best option for where to rest our hope. We worship, we pray, we study the Word of God, because those things feed our hope. They bring a redeeming quality to an otherwise struggling life. When you say you're saved, what you mean is not just that you've converted or you have a placed reserved in glory. When you say you're saved that means what causes other people to despair, you respond in hope. When you're saved, you might get jolted, hit by the realities of life, but somewhere along the line, you have to shake yourself and decide you've got a hope in a God who has already left on record that no matter how bad a thing appears to be, He can turn it around.

The helmet of salvation first brings deliverance, a hope that God can get you out. One dimension of salvation is to hope that, whatever in life has you in a place where you feel stuck or imprisoned, God can get you out. Stand on the frontline nailed to the truth that you are saved by a God who can get you out. Nothing that holds you tight is stronger than God's ability to get you out.

I have a story to tell you, readers. In a church not far, a pastor used an impactful story to make this very point. The story goes that after a few of the usual Sunday evening hymns, the church's pastor slowly stood up and walked to the pulpit. Before he gave his sermon for the evening, he briefly introduced a guest minister who was in the service that evening. In the introduction, the pastor told the congregation that the guest minister was one of his dearest childhood friends and he wanted him to have a few moments to greet the church and say whatever the Lord put on his heart. With that, an elderly man stepped up to the pulpit and began to speak:

"A father, his son, and a friend of his son, were sailing off the Pacific coast. A fast approaching storm blocked any attempt to get back to shore. Waves were so high that, even though the father was an experienced sailor, he couldn't keep the boat upright. The boat capsized and the three were swept into the ocean."

The old man hesitated for a moment making eye contact with two teenagers who were in attendance and for the first time they were now paying attention. The aged minister continued.

"Grabbing a rescue line, the father had to make the most excruciating decision of his life. To which boy would he throw the other end of the lifeline? He only had seconds to make a decision. The father knew that his son was a Christian. He also knew that the son's friend was not. The agony of his decision could not be matched by the crashing of the waves. The father yelled out, 'I love you son!' and threw the lifeline to the son's friend. By the time the father had pulled the friend back to the capsized boat, his son had disappeared beneath the raging swells into the black of night and his body never to be recovered."

Suddenly, the two teenagers in the audience were sitting up straight, paying attention, and anxiously waiting for the next words to come out of the old minister's mouth. He continued.

"The father knew that his son would step into eternity with Jesus, but he couldn't bear the thought of his son's friend stepping into an eternity without Jesus. Therefore, he sacrificed his son to save his son's friend. How great is the love of God that He should do the same for us. Our Heavenly Father sacrificed His only son that we could be saved."

He closed his recitation, "I urge you to accept His offer to rescue you. Take hold of the lifeline the pastor is throwing out to you in the service."

With that, the old man turned and sat down in his chair. Silence filled the room. People looked ambivalent, almost upset. The pastor walked slowly to the pulpit, delivered his brief sermon, and the invitation was extended. One person responded to the appeal. Within minutes following the service, the two teenagers jumped up from the pew, walked over to the old man and said to him, "That was a nice story, but I don't think it was realistic for a father to give up his only son's life in hopes that the other boy would ever become a Christian." The old man said, "Well you have a point." Glancing down at his old Bible, a big smile broadened his narrow face. He once again looked at the boys in their eyes and said, "You're right. It sure doesn't seem very realistic, does it? But I'm standing here tonight to tell you that story gives us a glimpse of what it must have been like for God to give up His son. You see, I was the father, and your pastor is my son's friend." Realistic or not, God can deliver you out of some things if you can have Him controlling the center of the mind.

The helmet of salvation is believing God, not only for deliverance out of, but for believing God for safety while going through all of life's challenges. Salvation brings a hope in the safety of God. This concentrates not on God getting you out; instead, this concentrates on God protecting you through. God will not always deliver you out of everything. Some things you have to go through on your own and endure what the experience has to offer—good or bad. What salvation gives, however, is a hope that if God doesn't get you out, God keeps you safe while you're going through. It's spiritually infantile to live with an expectation that God is always, when we're facing trial and attack, obligated to get us out. God wants witnesses going through life's challenges to testify to people going through the same, later. Everybody can't be out calling back to people going through, because they don't have as much incentive when you are over your stuff as when they can hear somebody still going through theirs but loving Jesus.

God wants witnesses going through life's challenges to testify to people going through the same, later.

I have one more story, readers, to hit home this often difficult concept.

An elderly woman found in her freezer a Butterball turkey. The problem was, it was 26 years old. She pulled it out, and, on it, was a 1-800 hotline number to call for Butterball Turkey. She called them, because she didn't like throwing anything away and wanted to know if she could still use it. When the customer service rep answered the phone, the woman asked, "Is it okay for me to thaw out and cook a turkey that's been in the freezer for 26 years?" The customer service rep responded, "Ma'am, if it was properly stored and adequately wrapped, it might be okay. But I wouldn't recommend it in light of how long it has been in the freezer." The old lady said, "Well I don't like to waste anything so whether or not the turkey is good or not, I'll give it to the church." Intentions were good here, but who knows how the innocent recipient of that turkey fared! And, what this humorous story tells you is that God will protect you from dangers—both seen and unseen—no matter what the underlying intentions are and no matter how grave the consequences can potentially be.

Salvation is not only deliverance out of and safety going through life, but preservation to bring us out to be the best we can be. Deliverance is God getting us out. Protection is God giving us safety while we're going through some of life's most difficult challenges. Here is the part we Christians need to anchor our future aspirations on: When I say I am saved, I am also anchoring a hope that God can preserve me while under attack so that there is quality to what I look like when it's over. We'll all struggle at some point. It's important, however, that we not only get out, but that we also look the part—look and sound like we struggled and learned and grew in salvation and faith.

THIRD INSTALLMENT:

A TESTIMONIAL TO THE ARMOR OF GOD

As parents, I know we all experience a variety of challenges in life. We worry about our kids, for example, from the day they are born until the day they leave home for college or work and beyond. Many times, we find ourselves trying to protect them, shield them, guide them, and even control them a bit. And, further, when it comes to the people in our children's lives, we want to control them too. After all, we raised this child, and we know this child—no matter what age he or she is, we still feel responsible for that child. Reining these feelings in and allowing our children to grow and become who they need to be is sometimes one of those life's challenges.

A friend of mine recently sent his youngest child off to college and, around the same time, welcomed home from college graduation his oldest. I could tell that he missed the younger of the two very much, since he had him home with him the whole time his big sister was away at school, and I could also tell that he was re-acclimating to life with his oldest, a daughter, who had developed some opinions of her own while away at school, was on a very directed job hunt, and had a boyfriend, with whom she was getting very serious.

My friend would often talk about how he missed his son and called him daily. He would get emotional talking about how there was a hole in his evenings where the boy's sports participation used to fill. My friend was open about how he was making some upgrades to his son's room—new blinds, a trendy chair, a new carpet and desk—all for when his son came home for the holidays or other school breaks. By contrast, he talked occasionally about how his daughter was staying in the guest room, having decided to move all of her belongings from her room to an apartment a couple years ago. He bristled over the fact that, now, jobless and trying to find her way, she was back in the house, more fixated on her resume than on having dinner with the family or helping out around the house.

I would listen to all of this and remember how, only four short years before, he had missed this daughter. I knew, in my heart, that he was still missing her in a way. He had sent off a high schooler with dreams of graduating from college, making new friends, and starting an exciting new life, and he got back a self-assured young lady with opinions that differed from his own and…with a new important man in her life—her boyfriend, who was very close to her. I tried to talk to him about his mixed feelings, but he didn't seem to want to disclose anything to me. Instead, I would listen as he complained about her job interview choices, and I would nod in understanding as he relayed his frustration over this new guy in her life—how he tried to "bribe" he and his wife with an expensive bottle of wine at dinner one night or how he bragged about his own family and their success and accomplishments. In my mind, I knew that this young man was just trying to impress my friend and his wife and that this was probably a sure sign that he was interested in a continued, positive relationship with the daughter and…that all of this was fantastic. I knew, however, that my friend didn't want to hear that right now. He was experiencing his own right of passage—that of a father letting his nearly grown kids go to lead their own lives and explore their own futures. I knew this was hard for him—no matter how fantastic or positive it appeared to those of us on the outside.

One day, my friend came to me and said that he had decided to tell his daughter that she would not be taking the job she was offered in a city about five hours away nor would she continue to see her boyfriend, who already had a job in that same city. I asked him why he was making such decisions, and he was unable to articulate why. He just shook his head and mumbled something about that crazy city and the disrespectful boyfriend. Because he was in a jovial mood otherwise, I attempted a conversation on the topic with him. To my surprise, he was ready to listen to my perspective, as an objective bystander, and to discuss his feelings as well.

We talked about how he had raised these kids with joy, strength, faith, and honesty. I reminded him that, if anyone knew the value of God's Armor and all that it entailed, these kids of his certainly did. They were hard working, loving, honest, and directed kids. Instead of feeling betrayed by his daughter and her drive to find a good job or upset that she had found a nice young man to love, he should be grateful and enjoy and embrace his blessings. And, while it was hard to let his youngest go— his only son—that God had done the same and expected, from us, as faithful, honest, and hard-working fathers, that we continue this journey in our own blessed lives.

I wasn't sure how he was going to take this frank discussion, but, to my surprise again, his mood improved. He sat for minute, deep in thought, then looked at me and said, "I've been blind to my own Armor. After a lifetime of living faithfully and trusting God, I wasn't able to trust my own children to handle their lives as they see fit. I raised them well, and I should be proud. I should also expect great things from them and embrace their honesty, their drive, and their love." Instead of responding right away, I listened, and I reminded myself that, when I inevitably would go through the same with my child in a number of years, that I would, also, remember to breathe and draw on my own strength to let these children of faith, equipped with God's Armor, to soar and live the blessed lives to which they were entitled.

SEVEN:

THE SWORD OF THE SPIRIT

Ephesians 6:17

"Take the helmet of salvation and sword of the Spirit, which is the word of God." (NIV)

THE SWORD OF THE SPIRIT

Drawing on our past chapters, Paul knows, when he sees that strange blade in the soldier's possession, exactly what it means. He knows that not every conflicting engagement this soldier faces is executed at a comfortable distance. Paul knows that, at times, the enemy will attack up close and personal. Paul reminds us that we will, at times, be too close in the attack to shield, block to defend, or to deflect. Sometimes when Satan attacks, your only option will be to engage. Don't ignore that! At some point, the battle is coming to a close. It won't be an attack on position, possessions, or placement, because while these are things that matter, they are not essential. The attack will, instead, be around the very essentials like identity—and not just who you are, but who you are attempting to be—who you have built—who you see as the definition of your being— what you know, how you feel, how you pray, and how you interact with others. The attack will also make you question everything relating to intimacy, your values, your ideas, your dreams, and your emotions.

When Satan brings the spiritual fight this close, Paul says it's time for us to fight. He says we all need the Spirit as a sword, used by the individual, through the Word of God. To fully understand how aggressive Paul is about this close combat engagement, he uses the word sword in this text, not to describe an elongated blade, but rather a short dagger—a curved blade, just 20-24 inches long—much like someone would pull intending to use right up close and intending to kill, before the attacker can do the same. This is big, because what he is suggesting is that this sword, or dagger, is for a strong strike for a fatal blow. You can't inflict damage to an adversary with this from a distance, but you pull it when you know the conflict is going to be engaged in tight quarters, close space, and with deadly intent—upon you, your values, your relationships, and your life. And we all know that, regarding faith, deadly intent can simply mean that the enemy is undermining us—killing or stopping anything positive that we set into motion or make part of our lives.

Sometimes when Satan attacks, your only option will be to engage.

The apostle Paul, has been very diligent about teaching us how to protect ourselves, how to intercept and extinguish those things that the enemy aims and releases in our direction. The helmet is to protect. The breastplate is to protect. The shield is to protect. Girded loins are to protect mobility. Shoes prepared are to protect space and territory. Being a disciple of Jesus Christ is not just about protecting yourself from the enemy in anticipation of the attacks he will send; being a disciple is also about doing damage to the enemy when space and time and circumstances demand it. Being a Christian is not only about learning to spiritually respond to life but also to be intentional and aggressive about how you make spiritual progress, how you grow, how you advance, and how you produce.

Paul is teaching here that we are never expected to just absorb and take everything all the time. With attacks, temptations, intrusions, invasions, assaults, and bombardments, we are not expected to just defend ourselves all the time; that would be emotionally, spiritually, and even physically exhausting. Blocking, extinguishing, deflecting, and intercepting are all strenuous tasks—whether they are physical or just emotional and spiritual. We have limitations, and we are not expected to negotiate all the time. There comes a time, however, when the enemy attacks, that God absolutely expects you to strike back.

The difference between investing in safety when it is about the shield, helmet, and the breastplate, and engaging the strike with the sword, is contingent upon where and how Satan has determined to bring the fight to you. When Satan is attempting to attack from a distance, defend! When Satan is determined to bring the attack up close, Paul suggests that you have something to help you strike back, swiftly, effectively, and decisively. Close spiritual combat demands more than just praying about it and more than just waiting on God to do something about it. At times, it requires that you be willing to see your spirituality as giving you the support and strength you need to not let Satan dominate your personal space. You can't always strike with the dagger when he is attacking with something that the swing of the dagger can't cut. You have to be able to assess your situation from a position of strength.

When Satan is attempting to attack from a distance, defend.

We all know, or think we know, when we've been tested. This is how Satan thrives. And, he knows what truly affects us. Sometimes, we think he is affecting us, but, really, we can all handle attacks on our peripheral realities—surroundings, money, and material possessions. When he attempts attacks there, we aren't moved as much, because he's not really touching US. We can intercept and extinguish the fire when Satan releases these flaming arrows at what we think is security; it is when he goes beyond and attacks us personally and spiritually that we are often left blindsided. At these times, Satan gets close enough to touch us—our ideas, our values, our dreams, self-esteem—the very rhythm of our heartbeats and the depth of our souls. When Satan gets that close—when the attack is starting to touch us and affect what we think about ourselves or affect how we imagine our worlds—even affect how we decide to make progress in our worlds, Paul says that's when we know it is time to fight.

What you do in the fight, however, must be swift, thorough, and decisive. Paul intimates here that this close spiritual combat engagement calls for the sword of the Spirit. This means all of us need a connection with the Spirit such that the enemy's attacks should not be for us all the time. These are elongated, protracted engagements. We shouldn't be fighting the devil about the same issue all the time. Don't let the devil stay in your life in a specific area affecting it for a long time. If you are a disciple of Jesus Christ, when you recognize the enemy has infected, and is affecting, a particular area, Paul says you have in your possession something that can determine how short that time is. The enemy is only given as much time as your inability to decide that you have had enough. When he brings it up close and personal, it is time to be swift and thorough and decisive.

This means all of us need a connection with the Spirit such that the enemy's attacks should not be for us all the time.

This is important for perfecting your spiritual disciplines. Spiritual discipline keeps us connected to our relationship with God. It helps us to develop spiritual instincts so that when you are faced with unfortunate, unwanted, or uninvited realities that shock and stagnate other people, you will instinctively respond with spiritual disciplines that keep you in the presence of God, in the will of God, and flowing under the protection of God. You ought to exercise your spiritual disciplines by saturating your life in prayer, focusing on immersion in the scripture, and remaining focused on worship. Above all this, we have to also have, as one of our spiritual disciplines, sensitivity to the Spirit, for which we have developed such a listening acuity that when the Spirit speaks, we know it is the Spirit. If we practice this, we will be able to differentiate from when the Spirit speaks and from when Satan is attempting to reach us or challenge us by mimicking and, therefore, sounding like the Spirit.

Remember, when the enemy has brought the battle up close and personal to the point that it is starting to touch and even affect your ideas, your values, and your self-worth, it should be imperative to engage in this battle—to fight—to use your spiritual fortitude—that image of the sword and your strength and protection—to offset Satan. Instead of Satan inflicting a wound on all of us in these cases, we should all be able to inflict a wound on him. Take note and stay strong in that when there is space between when Satan strikes and how long it takes you to respond, it is not always an indication that there is a lack of faith or you're in the throes of infantile righteousness or even that your trust being has been eroded. Take heart—trust in yourself and your faith; a pause or a moment of thought or even fear in addressing or facing these issues—these flaming arrows that Satan throws your way—might just mean that you just haven't trained yourself regarding how to use your offensive weapon, which is that dagger, that sword of the spirit, that strength. Paul only says that the Spirit is your close combat weapon. He reminds us all that the Spirit—that strength of faith—becomes our sword, which, ultimately, reminds us of the Bible's description of the sovereignty of your majestic God. It does take pause; it does require some reflection. Revel in that and use it for additional fortitude. Once it brings back to our remembrance of what God's Word has already taught us, it is easier to come to grips with the power of God in the earth, above the earth, and in the Heavens.

The Word is God's revelation of how His sovereignty is bent, with favor, in your direction. The Word is the art of war manual for the Christian for how to survive the battle and how to do damage to the enemy while you are surviving. God intended for you to walk in complete victory, to conquer, to excel, to progress, and to do it with a degree of spiritual providence. In order to do that, you will have to fight! You have to fight to define what God says He's called you to do. When you have determined that it is time to fight, nail yourself to the frontline, make sure your helmet is on, put the shield in your hand, cover up from the neck to the navel with your breastplate, wrap truth around your waist, and put your feet in ready-made shoes ready with the Gospel of peace. All of that is defense. When you are standing on the frontline and Satan decides to cross the line, pull the dagger out and do some damage.

You have to fight to define what God says He's called you to do.

One of the reasons the Spirit, for us, doesn't function as a sword is because we at times carry a faulty perception of the purpose of the Word. We think the Bible was written to help us know us, so we read it because we want from it something that helps us to know us. This is why scientists and church antagonists comb through ancient biblical territory trying to disclaim or discredit biblical facts. They try to find artifacts to confirm or deny the chronological accuracy as written in scripture. The Bible was not written to confirm chronological facts. The Bible was not written to show you yourself. The Bible was written for one purpose; to show you God. Coming to know the God of the Scripture helps you to suddenly know yourself and your role in creation, and faith, and the Word of God, because you don't know anything—and you can't know true spirit and faith—until you know God. The better you know God, the better you know you. Paul says that when Satan is attacking, the Spirit is feeding you the Word. If the Word's focus is to get you to see God, then when the Spirit is talking, it tells you that God is going to fight this battle for you.

The Bible was written for one purpose; to show you God.

The Philistines worshipped a half man/half fish god called Dagon. When they seized Israel, they took the arc of the covenant, a symbol of the very presence of God, and they sat it next to this god, Dagon. As the nation slept, Dagon was knocked from its pedestal in the temple, face down on the floor. The nation gets up the next morning, goes into the temple and sees Dagon on the floor. They pick Dagon up and put their god in place. The next night while the nation sleeps, Dagon is knocked off of the pedestal again. All that is left is its torso. No one had entered the temple on the two nights that Dagon was knocked from the pedestal. What happened is God knocked Dagon down and broke Dagon into pieces, because God doesn't exist next to anybody.

Sometimes the fight is just too close. You can't defend, you can't deflect, and you can't pray it away, but you can handle the close combat if the Spirit is your sword. Whatever Satan is bringing against any of us, we are standing, united in spirit, against him with one weapon, and that is the eternal Word of God.

EIGHT:

PRAYER AS THE ESSENTIAL ELEMENT

Ephesians 6:18

"And pray in the Spirit on all occasions with all kinds of prayers and requests. With this in mind, be alert and always keep on praying for all the saints." (NIV)

"Do all of this in prayer asking for God's help. Pray on every occasion, as the Spirit leads. For this reason keep alert and never give up; pray always for all God's people." (GNT)

PRAYER, THE ESSENTIAL ELEMENT

After spiritually clothing himself, the apostle Paul, sees the need for one more thing that is not directly observable on the soldier. What Paul says is important—that we, basically, need to fight in faith; however, he doesn't see this as apparent on the soldier. As you know, in these previous chapters, Paul has given to us what he does see and, for us, he has drawn the necessary spiritual parallels. You will recall that he says we need garments that are wrapped with a belt of truth, from the neck to the navel covered with a breastplate of righteousness, on the battlefield carrying the shield of faith to intercept and extinguish all flaming arrows. Our shoes should be ready to be nailed by the power of the gospel of Jesus Christ even if on the frontline of life's battles. We should have on us a helmet of salvation protecting the control center of the mind and finally the short dagger of the word of God should the confrontation call for close combat. This we know—this we have been over again and again as we examine this text.

So…Paul is looking at the soldier, and he accepts that has analyzed and understood every essential piece of armor or clothing that the soldier needs to execute his duties and to do so with the best chance of survival and guaranteed victory. He has translated this, for us, to life and how to live it. In fact, everything that Paul sees on the soldier he can parallel, for us, as disciples of the Lord Jesus Christ to ensure that we, too, go into spiritual warfare protected, armed, and mentally prepared—not only to just survive but to, if necessary, inflict damage and to come out the victor after the attack. Of course, while the soldier is truly prepared for a life and death battle, we know, after examining this text, in essence, with Paul, we are preparing for attacks on our psyche, our personal and prayer lives, and our faith.

As Paul ponders this idea that he cannot actually see the faith on this soldier—this guy who absolutely needs faith in fellow soldiers or in himself—he begins to think more deeply, beyond just the surface. Paul, in his introspection and to our benefit, finally realizes the essential element that the disciple of the Lord needs to ensure that the other pieces of the spiritual armor are maximized, and he sees it initially, as we all would, as thought or introspection. Again, Paul doesn't see anything overtly on the soldier, but he knows that faith needs to be in the life of every disciple, and he knows that this additional component to tie it all together is probably only present in a true disciple. Wrestling in the spiritual life against satanic presence demands that the pieces of armor that a disciple wears—a soldier in this battle against opposing forces—are maximized by alert prayer. Of course, this is the missing element! We all know that, especially in times of strife, battle, or stress, we pray, and we truly wear our faith on our respective sleeves. Unfortunately, for far too many, it is an essential missing element. They have protected the control center of the mind. They have wrapped themselves in the truth of God's sovereign existence. They are covered from neck to navel with a heart determined to live under God's divine authority. They are nailed to the frontline of the battle believing the gospel of Jesus Christ to be the power of God unto salvation. They intercept and extinguish flaming arrows with a firm resolute, fixed, determined belief in a sovereign God. They have quick access to the close combat short dagger of the Lord when Satan brings the attack up close and personal. They have not, however, taken the time to refine their faith or protect and polish their prayer lives. They have not made their prayer defense impenetrable. They remain, instead, vulnerable and, many times, uneducated when it comes to what they should do when Satan tries to approach any of us in prayer or in intellectual repose.

If we listen, we can tell that Paul instructs us by saying that having done all of this makes us all absolutely ready to fight—getting the armor in place—preparing the outside for the attacks of the unknown. The question remains, however, are we all ready to fight at our best? If we are ready to fight at our best spiritually, and, if we do have a strong prayer life, we are, as Paul says, ready for that last key component. Only the disciple of the Lord has access to this final piece; as we discussed, this last piece is that we must be practiced and alert in prayer—always.

The question remains, however, are we all ready to fight at our best?

When the enemy attacks in any occasion, Paul tells us that we need to respond by praying in the power of and in the sphere of the Spirit with intensity to our prayers. We need to remember to be persistent about prayer on every occasion—when we find ourselves on the spiritual battlefield, and…even when we find ourselves blessed and calm in our lives. Only the truly protected and faithful are found on the battlefield, unscathed, fully dressed and alert in prayer.

Paul says that we can't be selfish about our prayers because, at this level of discipleship responsibility, we are all beyond just praying for ourselves. We, at this stage, are also obligated to pray for others, particularly those who are on our side, because Satan might be able to get to a soft spot in your life through a weak spot in another person's life. We have all experienced times when children, friends, spouses, or co-workers have brought us into something that we would normally not pursue. Maybe we are tempted to cheat on something at work because of a team member's urging or maybe one of our kids has gotten into trouble or prompted us to act inappropriately or our or character in their defense. With these people and regarding these relationships in our lives, we have to consider that perhaps there is a piece of armor that they don't have or they might be missing the element of prayer in their lives. And, as much as we might resist or try to do the right thing, we become injured or compromised because our fight is strong but theirs is weak, or they are not as committed as we are, as faithful Christians steeped in prayer and the necessary Armor of God. We don't want to find ourselves becoming injured because someone close to us wasn't as committed to the fight as we are, not as fully dressed for the battle as we are, not as focused for the fight as we are, or not as hungry to fight strong as we are. Paul says that we all better pray about that battle, not just for how we will fight when the time comes, but we all need to pray for the continued strength to fight for those who won't or can't.

Paul suggests that prayer, for those of us who are evolved Christians, expands in definition. Prayer is no longer just simply the channel and method of communication with God for us. And this is something that is important to note. Prayer is not just maintaining our spiritual relationships, giving us ways to talk to God, so we can then silence our spirits, turn off the noise of the culture and other distractions, so God can speak to us and so that we can speak to God. Paul makes us aware that prayer is a piece of spiritual warfare equipment. He tells us that, while we are praying to maintain a channel of clear communication with God and while we are praying to maintain a spiritual healthy relationship with God, even while we are praying to talk to God and waiting for God to talk back to us, prayer also becomes a weapon on the battlefield. It is to ensure that we fight spiritual warfare with the best chance of coming out victorious. Paul tells us to pray persistently, keeping ourselves in the power of the Spirit or the sphere of the Spirit, because it makes us quicker to rightly respond to Satan's angle of attack, his method of attack, his instrument of attack, who he intends to use to attack, and his timing of attack. In other words, we can't always see what's coming, but we know what to do when a catastrophic event in life sends us something negative to handle. If we remain strong, we can take natural disasters, loss of job, temptations to stray from our faithful path, or enticements to take the easy way to success or to lie and cheat. We can pray, maintain our strength, and protect all that we have built in our armor to keep Satan away and our own positive track or pathway in life in mind.

And, all of this is what helps us to grow from responding because we were attacked, to responding because we knew that we were going to be attacked. We are able to approach issues and challenges in a proactive, prepared way as opposed to reactive and angry way. Being prepared in this way allows us to provide a quick counterstrike and a defensive protection plan because, not only do we know that Satan is getting ready to attack our lives in certain areas, but if we persistently praying in our daily lives, we also are given an insight into the weapon he is going to us, how he is going to advance, the force behind what he's using, and God's intended strategy to make sure we come out on the other side. Praying allows us to truly meditate and focus on what we hold close as strengths, what fears we need to cast aside, and just how much is riding on our ability to perform in these instances. After all, part of knowing how to react comes from understanding the blessings we have and the power behind our faith and the lives that we have built, flaws, problematic relationships and all.

We are able to approach issues and challenges in a proactive, prepared way as opposed to reactive and angry way.

114

If we're honest with ourselves, we will admit that prayer helped us to know some things that had we not prayed, we would have never known about them—these strengths, fears, needs, hopes, and more. Prayer helped us to prepare for things in life that we may not have known otherwise—how to take care of a baby, how to rise above the death of a loved one, or even how to study and work towards certain goals beyond our current experience. Prayer helped us survive some people that would have ruined our lives previously—difficult bosses, family members who have gone astray, others who, for whatever reason, decide they don't like us or want to include us. Prayer got us mentally prepared because we had time after praying to adjust, to rely on God, to trust His presence, to trust that He had your back. It is hard, as responsible people, at times, to trust that God is covering our lives, to trust that God puts favor upon us, or to trust that God had a purpose for what any of us were going through during trying times in our lives. If none of what has happened to us makes sense, then at least we can trust that God was there, through all these confusing or deeply troubling times from which it appear there was no escape; in all these times, God was going to protect, and God was going to deliver us to the other side. Without the essential element of prayer, we are always recovering from an attack. Even if we survive it, we're always recovering. With the essential element of prayer, we are actively countering the attack as we pray and expect challenges because we can see, in our prayer life, that God will actually tell us what is coming or what can come to challenge all that we know and love.

Let's hypothetically suggest two combatants hit the octagon, both of equal physical capability, same height, same weight, same reach, same experience, and same amount of wins and losses. What provides a point of departure is which fighter has trained, not only his physicality but also his spirituality. Not only is he able to go into the octagon and win because he's physically strong, but he's able to win because he's spiritually strong. He can read the opponent's move before the opponent makes the move, and he is able to counter before the opponent fully executes the move. It shocks the other person. Being alert in prayer makes you intentional about the way you live. You must believe me when I say that, if you are vigilant in your prayer life, you're not responding to life accidentally. When you know Jesus, you are not living by accident; you are living under God's divine providence. You wake up in the morning knowing that beyond anything else, God's providence is going to be manifested in your life. Nothing is by accident; everything is by providence.

If you are vigilant in your prayer life, you're not responding to life accidentally.

In our text here, Paul is suggesting that we are faced with the question that can only be answered by committing ourselves to going to our battles with the essential element of consecrated prayer. Paul tries to warn all of us that one of the reasons we need to go to the battle with prayer is simply because we are going to the battle. In fact, he tells us that every day, we are wrestling in the spiritual realm. There are times when the devil will wrestle with us through people, but there are other times, as Paul says, that you wrestle not against flesh and blood but against spirits and principalities and spiritual wickedness in high places. Paul warned you that Satan will try to shoot arrows for you from a distance. He is going to tip the arrow in pitch and set it on fire because, if it can't strike a vital organ, he wants to enflame something in your life. All of these well-lived and good-intentioned lives can be lost to Satan if we are not vigilant in our prayer life. All that we work for and strive for can be questioned, attacked, and taken from us with the wrong moves or the wrong path to handling any challenges that come our way. We can't give in to destructive tendencies and habits, and we cannot make dire mistakes that put our families, ourselves, and our livelihoods in trouble, simply because we're attacked from outside. And, we can't be fooled into thinking that there is no recovery from incidents or challenges because there is, and, through prayer, we are capable of coming back from anything.

All that we work for and strive for can be questioned, attacked, and taken from us with the wrong moves or the wrong path to handling any challenges that come our way.

Paul also tells us how Satan is going to come. He's going to come through tricks and schemes and wiles. He is going to attack us in whatever area we have left a vulnerable opening, whether that's in your heart, your mind, your emotions, or your situations. It may be through vulnerabilities, events, disappointments, or through blind spots, and any other way that would provide him just enough entrance into your life so that when he gets in there, it his hope to deaden your faith, injure your spiritual ambition and make you abandon obedience for disobedience. The good news is that you don't have to fall for it. You don't have to trip over it. You don't have to be halted by it. You don't have to be stagnated by it. You don't have to be depressed about it. You just have to be determined to fight. The enemy sometimes makes us all fight things that have nothing to do with us pushing forward in life and making things right or staying the path to success. It is the enemy that has you continuing to think about a life that God doesn't even intend for you. God's got all power and wants you to wrap your motivations, energy and dreams in prayer so that he can take you to the battlefield ready put up the good fight of faith. There is no reason to dwell on what you can't do or mistakes that you've made when you know what you can accomplish and how blessed and strong your life and actions can be.

We already know we are going to have to fight. The question is not if you're going to fight. The question is how do you want to fight? What sphere do you want to be immersed in when the attack comes? Do you want to be on the battlefield hoping God is going to show up or do you want to be on the battlefield knowing you are coming under power? When you know you are going in under the covering of the blood of Jesus you will not lose. Paul says if you want to fight strong then don't just worry about all of the external things but consecrate yourself in prayer. When you walk in the sphere of the Spirit your vision sharpens. Your reflexes are quicker. Your sensitivities are sharpened so that not only do you know the enemy is going to attack, but also you know the angle of attack he is going to send. When you get to a place in the spirit you can relax, rely and respond because God will have shown you what was coming and the response then will minimize damage and guarantee a right response.

Do you want to be on the battlefield hoping God is going to show up or do you want to be on the battlefield knowing you are coming under power?

Let me illustrate. In the bible, we can all recall that, in another text, Joseph gets the coat of many colors his father gives him because he is the chosen child. He has these dreams that he is going to be superior in later days over all of his brothers. He makes the mistake of sharing his dreams with his brothers. They decide they need to get rid of him. Joseph is then taken to Egypt, and for 20 years, his life goes into an unfortunate, unwanted tailspin. Because he had a dream that God was going to allow him to occupy a place and purpose in the kingdom, no matter what happens to him in between when the dream is given and the dream is realized, he lives bases on what he sees and not what he sees. When Joseph gets out of jail, where he ultimately ends up, his brothers are concerned about what method of revenge he will exact upon them. Joseph, however, understands that, what they meant for evil, God used it for his good. He saw it 20 years ago and acted on what he saw, not what they had done. He lives in the way God wants him to live, and he does not follow the path shown to him by his brothers, who have done wrong. And, we can all relate to this. Many times, in life, we are challenged to exact revenge on people who have wronged us or tried to harm us, but we have to turn the other cheek and take the high road. It can be frustrating at times, but we know, as disciples of God, that the best path is the one that involves prayer, discipline, and strength in maintaining our own lives, protecting family, or bettering ourselves—not one that involves revenge, inappropriate behavior, and a reactionary attitude.

In our current text, Paul is offering us now another layer of gratitude for God being in our lives. For the most part, we live grateful to God because having God present in our lives makes us able to function and excel every day. God knows ability alone is not enough. Paul tells us that after we are made sufficiently able to fight, God wants to make us aware. When awareness and wed to ability, we won't have to be caught by surprise.

For the most part, we live grateful to God because having God present in our lives makes us able to function and excel every day.

To give you another real life example, let's say that a criminal wants to break into your house. You keep a big stick in the basement. You are upstairs in the bedroom, and the criminal breaks in. Your ability is in the basement and you can't get to it because you had no awareness that you were going to need it. The criminal trips over a bush while trying to break in and makes you aware that he is breaking into the house. Now your awareness forces or causes you to actively reach out for your ability. My message to you is this: Don't leave your awareness in the basement or your ability in the basement. Take both of them wherever you go and, if you do this whenever Satan shows up, God will let you know that he's coming, and you can show your ability and stand up to him, stopping or lessening the attack on your life and on the lives of those you love.

This is critical to understand because every other piece of the armor speaks to ability. Every other piece of the armor helps us to become able to defend, to inflict damage, to protect, to advance, and to survive. Only prayer gives you awareness so that your ability can be matched with awareness, which, of course, then means if we persistently pray in the Spirit, on all occasions, being alert, praying for others, we enter a sphere in the Spirit in which we not only see what God sees, but we see it before we see it. In other words, we learn how to anticipate challenges and how to gauge, ahead of time, how we will react. From there, it is just a matter of execution. We know what to do; we just have to wait, prepared, for the attack. There is never a moment where God is not aware of what is about to take place. God sees from eternity, and eternity has no first day when He saw; He sees everything. Every day of eternity is always in God's mind. God sees things in your life down the road but He saw it from eternity past, which means when it happens, it never catches God by surprise because He has known forever what lies in wait for all of us. If we live with persistent prayer and radical obedience, whatever God allows in your "right now" is because He already saw how He was going to use it in your "not yet." So, in essence, our plan is laid into place, and it won't be without challenges, but it will be a path that we can all handle and for which we were meant. Prayer can help us, not only keep the attacks under control, but it can allow us the ability to see our own talents and to tap into our own strengths, blessings, and opportunities. Some of us need God to remind us that, while some things have not happened yet, we can walk in them like they already have happened since He knows what's in store for us and knows we can, not only just handle it, but come out better for it all—challenges, low points, and all.

In other words, we learn how to anticipate challenges and how to gauge, ahead of time, how we will react.

Imagine how different your decisions would have been if, through prayer, you had seen a situation before you walked it. When you commit to dressing your inside reality with persistent prayer, you can live so spiritually sensitive that everyday God makes you aware of your context so much so that you know how to function not by reacting but by expecting.

Football player, Deion Sanders, was asked once during an interview how he had become so quick on the ball. He replied that over the years he had developed an awareness of how to read the quarterback before he even took the snap. As the quarterback was backing up looking in the opposite direction, he knew he was going to throw over there and got to the spot before the receiver did. When the ball would come, all he would need to do was step in front and take the pass. Using this mentality and careful study of our own situations, we wouldn't have to keep fighting Satan to get some of our blessings if we would learn how to be aware of where God is going to be dropping them. You don't have to wait for someone else to deliver it; you just have to be obedient to get where God is. Pastor, scholar, author, and poet, Eugene Peterson, said, "Show me where you're working and let me join you there."

We all know the story, in the Bible, of how Moses is called by God to go back to Egypt and stand before Pharaoh and tell him to let His people go. Moses said he couldn't because he stuttered. God tells him to go and that He is his sure defense. Pharaoh tells him he will not let them go. Moses does not run from the confrontation because God also, with ability, gave him awareness of the totality of the deliverance plan. He told him that Pharaoh was not going to let him go the first time, but it will be after ten plagues. Moses goes multiple times. He does not run, and just starts counting. After the ninth plague, the next morning, Pharaoh lets the people go. If Moses had left after the second denial, he would not have been around to watch and lead Israel in the exodus, but he persisted, and he prevailed.

Moses does not run from the confrontation because God also, with ability, gave him awareness of the totality of the deliverance plan.

When Jesus, near the end of his life, sat with the disciples in the upper room, he tells them that one of them will betray Him. So little was the evidence of whom it was that each of them said, "Is it me?" Why did they ask if it was one of them when not one of them had confessed to each other that they were even wrestling with it? Had they confessed, the others would have said who it was. Judas asks, as the others did, if it was him. Jesus tells him, "yes," and tells him to go do what he will do. Judas ponders this, and, we all know that Jesus does tell him what will transpire, and he goes forth and does just what he is meant to do, setting, of course, a whole chain of events into action, all events that Jesus knew would happen.

In the same text, Peter is listening to Jesus describe how He is going to die. Peter is telling Jesus that they will fight for Him and will fight for Him to the death. Jesus tells Peter that he sees something in his future and that, before the rooster crows three times, Peter will deny Him. The difference between Peter and Judas is Judas runs out, sells Jesus out anyway and, because there is no attachment of any promise on the other end, Judas has no ambition to live and hangs himself. Peter is in the courtyard warming his hands by the fire and sees Jesus being led from one court to another. Jesus looks him in his eyes and the scripture says that Peter remembers what Jesus said. He remembered that Jesus said, "Satan desires to sift you as wheat, but I have prayed for you, and when you are converted..." Because Jesus saw him converted, Peter repented and lived what Jesus saw. When God makes you aware, you don't live by your evidence, you live by what God shows you that is on His mind concerning you. You live anticipating that what God has shown you; He won't let you die before it comes true because God's Word will not lie.

God wants you able and He wants you aware. You exercise that in three ways: Pray constantly, pray intensely, and pray unselfishly. It is said that the other pieces of the armor is your equipment but prayer is your energy. We win because God gives up equipment, but He also gives us energy, the Spirit. As we pray persistently, the Spirit becomes our energy.

FOURTH INSTALLMENT:

A TESTIMONIAL TO THE ARMOR OF GOD

When I was a very young man, attending grade school, I had a wide variety of people I called my friends. A number of them were academically great, and others struggled a bit. Some were very athletic, and others had not yet found their niche sport. Still others were social, while some in our little group were not. I was somewhere in the middle of all that, and, I still feel to this day, relatively sensitive about the needs of my friends—their challenges—their triumphs. I felt we were all a pretty close group of kids.

As we got older and into middle school, my friends and I all came into our own a bit. Some of us did gravitate towards athletics—some even became "stars" on our school's basketball and football teams. Others became scholars—and still others just maintained a diversity, a balance of interests and mischievousness that made them who they were too. We all remained close friends and spent a lot of time together—presumably through all of our ups and downs in our pre-teen and teenage lives.

One day, as we were all discussing an upcoming school dance, I noticed that one of the group was holding back a bit—not contributing to the conversation and not acting as excited or as happy as the rest of us. He declined to discuss his morose mood with us, but I noticed that, over the next few weeks, his mood got worse. And, honestly, as I observed him and watched him, I noticed that he often held back. I noticed, too, that he was often very shy and, further, that when anyone challenged him, he had trouble standing up for himself. In other situations, these challenging situations turned into, what I considered at the time, minor bullying incidents. He would encounter other kids who dominated him or even made fun of his shyness, his constantly downcast eyes and his reluctance to speak up for himself, and he would tense up and retreat—pick up his lunch tray or his books and leave or find another seat in whatever room we were sitting. I realized, as I continued to observe more closely, that I hadn't noticed this dynamic before. I had not even realized that a close friend of mine was suffering and might need help.

As the day for the dance loomed, I decided to approach my friend about two things. One—I wanted to tell him that I had his back when the kids I observed started to bug him. And, two—I wanted to know why the dance was upsetting him so much. I waited until we were alone at lunch, safely at an out of the way table where no one would bother us. With me, he was always jovial and friendly, and I didn't want to ruin his mood. I tentatively approached the subject of the bullying, and he was open to discussion about it. He told me that he was relieved that I would stand up for him and…that he was happy that someone close to him finally noticed. He regarded the bullies as "annoyances"—not people who could actually hurt him at all. However, when I brought up the dance, he went silent, and his face changed. I had obviously unintentionally touched a nerve.

He proceeded to tell me that, when my friends and I talked to our peers or other girls, it hurt him that the girls rolled their eyes at him or that the bullies made him seem weak—uninteresting—someone to laugh at or ignore. In his mind, he was smart and hard-working, proud of his accomplishments at school whether or not he was on the honor roll; he just liked being in the science club, because he enjoyed it—and he liked mixing with other like-minded students. And, while he wasn't on a sports team, he liked playing basketball with us after school and never questioned the fact that we would include him or not. When these other people—all kids who did not know him as well as we, the tightknit group from grade school, did—picked on him or disregarded him, he felt ashamed and sad. He told me that they made him question everything about himself—that maybe he wasn't welcome in science club—or maybe we all laughed at him after he left our friendly basketball games. He confided that they all made him feel differently about himself—like he was nothing—like he was someone he didn't even know himself. With the dance looming, he felt that he couldn't even approach a girl to go— and…might not even go himself if he was that different than others or unwelcome in social situations. In his mind, he was fine, but…in these uncomfortable, bullying environments, he felt challenged, different, and compromised in terms of who he was or thought he was.

At the time, my friends and I simply took up for him more often— noticed when he felt left out—and his confidence and state of mind improved. In hindsight, as an adult, the story has stuck with me along with the feelings I had listening to him confide his insecurities—all brought on by other people. He and I are still friends to this day, and, while we never talk about our chat that day, I know he still thinks about it too. I know, because he holds his sword of the spirit strong at all times. He strategically swings or jabs when he knows that his very sense of self or what he feels is the life that makes him comfortable are threatened. He is polite and gracious—only striking when he knows that Satan and all his tricks are at work. He applies this to his job, his personal life, and his daily interactions in the community. He is a leader, someone we all look up to—and…he seems to have the knowledge that only one with a background in doubt—for no good reason—has. He has risen above self-doubt all because, long ago, he learned how to apply and use the sword of the spirit.

NINE:

BECOMING AN AMBASSADOR TO ALL

Ephesians 6:19-20

"¹⁹Pray also for me, that whenever I speak, words may be given me so that I will fearlessly make known the mystery of the gospel, ²⁰for which I am an ambassador in chains. Pray that I may declare it fearlessly, as I should." (NIV)

AMBASSADOR IN CHAINS

Paul is expressing here, in this text, the strange context he finds himself in, and he is not holding back his personal perception of it. In his mind, he is asking the question, what is he, an ambassador, doing chained like this to a Roman soldier? This is how Paul views himself, as an ambassador of the kingdom of God, sent to express the political ambitions and spiritual desires of another, in this case, God. The political ambition and spiritual aim of the One Paul represents is to include the Gentiles in the worshipping and witnessing community of those who live to honor the God of Abraham, Isaac, and Jacob. This political agenda and this spiritual desire have both become accessed because of the good news of the life, death, burial, and resurrection of Jesus. Jesus' life provides the open access for those who were formerly rejected to live now accepted as part of God's beloved community. Paul, attempting to be faithful to his ambassadorial role, now wrestles, in this text, with the way he is being treated for simply sharing another's message or another's agenda. Paul says he is an ambassador and as an ambassador, by expectation, he feels he should be treated better than being chained to this Roman soldier. He should be immune to any such hostility even if he were representing any enemy kingdom, which we know Paul is not. However, Paul finds himself in chains in a hostile environment for surrendering to and living faithful to the mission to spread the good news of Jesus among conflicting people. He has accepted that ministry does not always bring popularity and faithfulness when it should and can actually create a context of struggle, conflict, and pain. To be the carrier of such good news, as is revealed in and through the life of Christ, can cause a strange ambiguity when one is treated so harshly. Paul finds himself fighting the temptation such a strange contradiction creates. And, as we know, thus far, in our examination of his interpretation of his captor's armor and how he translates it to what we need to do to arm ourselves for God, he is coming to terms with how to turn this predicament into something positive.

Jesus' life provides the open access for those who were formerly rejected to live now accepted as part of God's beloved community.

In this particular examination, what do we see as some of Paul's temptations? Paul has to be tempted to lessen the integrity of the message he preaches so that he might improve upon his personal condition; he must water the Gospel down, cheapen it, or soften it to appear more compliant or not as threatening to those who oppose him. He feels that if he waters the gospel down, it may lessen his own pain. He has to also be tempted to let the struggle of his context infect the passion of the message he is called to preach. After all, it's hard to be excited when you're preaching good news but from a bad place, so his position in the prison has affected how powerful, or not powerful, his message is. He has to be tempted to not use the message itself as a negotiating or bargaining chip for an improved condition. In other words, he must not become willing to sell the integrity of the message or to cheapen the integrity of the message in order to come to an agreement in which his condition would improve.

Paul worries about the possibilities of falling into such temptation. He carries such concern about this and has seen others already compromised by it that he just comes right out and asks the saints in Ephesus to pray for him, that he not be bitten by the temptation to the let the fear of what he is preaching and what it may mean for him personally as he aims to be faithful as an ambassador of the kingdom of God. Paul, in essence, says, "Pray for me, that I keep preaching fearlessly, boldly, and that I be faithful to the message of the kingdom agenda, anchored in the good news of a risen savior." Paul says he is an ambassador. Of all the descriptions and labels Paul could have attached to his life, he says, "I am an ambassador, dressed so as to identify the country I represent, adorned so as to point to the uniqueness and distinction of the country I represent, not ever present to represent my own interests but always present to represent the interests of the one who has sent me; to speak to the desires and wishes of the government I represent and to offer our government's presence and support and ambitions, bringing all of the power of that government to bear on who you are in hopes that it will make you a better people." In other words, Paul is saying that when he shows up, he is not pushing his agenda; he is pushing an agenda as an ambassador because he speaking on behalf of another.

We, too, are dressed and adorned, trained, and sent to be ambassadors of the kingdom of God. We are meant to change our look and our language when we are ambassadors for God. We are supposed to adjust ourselves to make sure that we are reaching who we want to reach. We must do this to ensure that we are completely understood because people should want to hear what is being shared as we represent the One who has sent us—just as Paul felt that he had to do whatever he could to get the Word of God to the people. There ought to be no sense of shame in our ambassadorial uniqueness and no shame in our looking different or sounding different. Further, we should have no shame in having a different agenda and being attached to a different loyalty. Everything about us ought to point to the difference Jesus makes in one's life, and we should be proud of how that sets us off from others. We are not called to fit in but, rather, we are called to present the other worldliness of the kingdom of God. God's kingdom is not trying to fit into the culture; God's kingdom is here to take over the culture. Like Paul, we know the joy of living representing the kingdom of God, the power it brings to one's life, the sense of purpose and fulfillment it provides, the gifts it creates in a person's life, the levels to which those gifts take a person, the peace of knowing your future is secure, your path is protected, and your agenda is secured. Unfortunately, we also know the temptations that are presented us when we are ambassadors of God's kingdom; they want us to do what our relationship with God doesn't sanction, allow, or permit. We worry that we will fall victim to the ease of such temptations or compromises, and, sometimes, we do.

We are meant to change our look and our language when we are ambassadors for God.

We all should know the struggle of knowing that every word we speak and every action we display really represent so much more than just us; the pressure we can sometimes put on ourselves when we consider that we are always representing the God of creation is something that we should relish, but it is something that others may try to compromise or change. Many people will tempt us to live differently, speak differently, and even deny all that we know. All of these attempts to make us stray from our path with God and our ability to spread His Word and maintain our ambassador qualities can make us all doubt, for sure, whether we want to relax some standards and be a little less concentrated on trying to be so faithful to God, or to do what improves your position, ensures your popularity, or advances your personal agenda. We understand what Paul says when he says, "Pray for me," because these temptations bite us all the time.

Many people will tempt us to live differently, speak differently, and even deny all that we know.

As a pastor, I want to be able to preach without fear and so I understand, firsthand, when Paul says that he wants to execute ministry without fear. We see him saying, basically, pray for me, because I can't tap people into the pathos of what I'm saying about God if, at the same time, everyone senses that I am fearful of what I am saying or fearful of how it will be interpreted or how it will be received. In my life, I can't help people see how fulfilling a life in Jesus is if while I'm preaching to them about a fulfilling life in Jesus, and I don't look like having Jesus in my life is fulfilling me at all. I can't get others to trade sorrow for joy if, when I present Christ to them, it looks like I slept with sorrow last night. If I want to get others excited about Jesus, I have to show up dressed like I'm excited, talking like I'm excited, acting like I'm excited, and offering what excites me. All of us have wrestled with this. We worry, at times, that our circumstances and how we handle them will contradict that faith we say we have in God. We don't want to say, act, or do something in a way that doesn't speak to who we truly believe God to be. We so want to represent God in our ambassadorial role so that people interpret His invitation right. We don't want people looking at us and saying, "If that's what following Jesus means, keep Jesus to yourself." We don't want to cheapen the integrity of God's kingdom invitation, so Paul says, "Pray for me" and you ought to be asking others to pray for you. This essentially is what Paul is praying and what all of us ought to intend in our spiritual pursuit as we seek to live as ambassadors of the kingdom of God.

Paul says, "Pray for me so that I may preach fearlessly, because I need to show no fear in places of peculiar juxtaposition." Juxtaposition means you put something side by side and what you hold up side by side can at times contradict each other. Paul says, further, "On the one side I am an ambassador, royalty, representing a government that has a king and I should be treated based on the level of respect offered to the king I am representing." On the other side, he says, "I am an ambassador in chains," one translation says "in bonds," so that "While I represent a government that should necessitate that I be treated with a certain kind of respect and favor, I am an ambassador chained to a Roman soldier. It's a strange juxtaposition; however, I can't trade in my ambassadorial responsibility because I don't like what I am attached to. I can't lessen what I am sent to share because I don't like where I am called to share it. I can't stop preaching because I don't like what preaching attaches to me. I have to be a Christian when it brings favor and when it brings suffering. Paul wrestles with this strange juxtaposition because he is the possessor of the treasure of the gospel of Jesus Christ, but instead of people treating it as good news, they are treating it like he is an enemy combatant. What has him perceived as an enemy is that he comes attached to Jesus. Paul says, "I don't ever want to let where I am affect what I am called to do while I am there. Just because I am going through doesn't mean I can't show someone that Jesus makes a difference in my life."

We are all trying to be serious as we walk as ambassadors in creation, wearing our "armor of God" and staying true to our own ambitions and the ambitions of God. We want to handle and execute our duties faithfully. The enemy knows that one of the things he can do to affect your pursuit to be faithful as God's ambassador is to get you confused about your juxtaposed realities and to get you arguing with God because you don't like where God has taken you. We touched on this in the previous chapter by exploring how the enemy will attack us. He will attack and attempt to move us from our own paths to success and our own paths in faith. Living a discipline prayer life helps with this. However, many of us still start thinking God is unfair, and we get confused and angry and perhaps bitter, embarrassed to show up. I'm here to say that if you're not careful, you'll sideline yourself because you'll think that if you belong to God that your condition ought to always be better. You might be tempted to put aside what you should be doing for the immediate satisfaction of something else when you know that living a clean, disciplined life in which you take care of family, strive for a good career, eat right and exercise, and even pray daily is right. In many ways, you and I have to go out in the world and be God's ambassadors to tell people in the world that you don't ever measure God by the stuff you have; you measure God by what God is doing on the inside. When the inside is strong and ready to fight that good fight, then the success and the good life will come.

> *I'm here to say that if you're not careful, you'll sideline yourself because you'll think that if you belong to God that your condition ought to always be better.*

When we are attempting to live for God, if we're not careful, the confusion of this ambassadorial role can provide an entry to the enemy until we start theologically wrestling with whether or not God is unfair. If we're honest, we can admit that we sometimes ponder, "God, when I got saved I didn't expect that I would deal with some of the things I have to deal with. I didn't expect that being a Christian would not eliminate some of my crises. I didn't expect that falling in love with Jesus would mean that so many people would fall out of love with me. It seems unfair. How can you make me an ambassador and then keep me chained to a soldier?" In other words, so many of us feel left out in doing God's work. We feel that opportunities and fun are passing us by. Sometimes, when we work so hard, we can't see that our lives and other lives of others are becoming better every day because of what we say, represent, or preach. If we stay confused about this, we can let confusion bleed into anger and anger into resentment until we start making mistakes in thought, actions and attitude. Paul says that this is not something we can just emotionally pull ourselves out of, so he says, "Pray for me, because I want to represent God well in the places of juxtaposition. I want to be faithful as an ambassador even if I am an ambassador in chains. I have recognized and I have affirmed that whatever God is doing doesn't always have to be about me. There are times when my predicament isn't about my comfort but about God advancing His agenda. There are times when my restrictions are not about my convenience but about where God needs me stuck so that He can get glory out of my life. Sometimes my issues are not because I want them. Sometimes my issues are so that God can have space and capacity for the manifestation of His work." That is the challenge of faith. That challenge is can you be consistent when things around you are inconsistent? Can you live with the same boldness when you're chained as you do when you're free? Can you live with the same boldness when you're sick as you do when you're well? Can you shout when you're working and shout when you're laid off?

Sometimes, when we work so hard, we can't see that our lives and other lives of others are becoming better every day because of what we say, represent, or preach.

Paul keeps announcing the otherworldly invitation of the kingdom while the people he's preaching to are trying to find some sure footing in the chaotic anxiety of a shifting culture. You and I have been called as ambassadors to be bold enough to stand in this place of historical crisis of the economy crumbling, a government attempting to redefine itself, neighborhoods being ravished, schools underfunded, families being attacked. You and I have to accept our ambassadorial responsibility to stand and fearlessly tell people that there is still much to celebrate. As a government redefines itself, and a church searches for how to present a message and offer ministry, not in prosperity but in scarcity, you and I should be bold enough to stand and declare there is no need to be depressed. In fact, you should be lifting up holy hands because, while the world is going through many challenges, the kingdom is sturdy. The economy of the kingdom is not suffering from any crisis. It is not attempting to redefine itself. Nobody is being laid off. The kingdom is moving strong. People are still being promoted. People are still being elevated. Ways are still being made. Supply is still coming and we are still living off of His riches. You better learn how to rely on the real government that is taking care of you. The government is upon His shoulders, and by His stripes, we have been healed.

The economy of the kingdom is not suffering from any crisis.

Paul says, "Pray for that I'm fearless when my context is juxtaposed. When I put up who I am in Christ next to what I'm going through, side by side, it doesn't seem that it's congruent. My job is to be bold, to talk about Jesus, when my juxtaposition seems polarized." Let's go a little deeper. He says, "Pray for me that I'm fearless preaching the message of the good news when the tool of my spiritual hermeneutic (method of interpretation) is my own disadvantage. Pray for me that when God puts me in place that I'll be able to exegete (to lift truth out of the text) truth from a place of disadvantage." Unfortunately, the opposite of exegesis is eisegesis, which means we dump something on the text. Some people are eisegetical pros; they make the scripture say what they need it to say. In those cases, however, they are not twisting scripture to fit their needs; they're twisting themselves to fit the scripture.

Let's put it all together. Paul says, "Pray for me that I be bold when my tool of interpretation is my own disadvantage and that when I'm in a disadvantaged place I can see truth rather than crave deliverance. I'm forced to interpret God's will for a Christian from being chained to a guard." The reason I'm offering this is because there would be no verses before 19 that spell out the spiritual armor if Paul were not chained to the soldier. Being chained gave to him and exegetical insight that he would not have got unless he was chained. Have you, at times, been surprised at the places where God showed himself to you? Have you been surprised at the stuff God took you through to teach you what you had been reading all along? Are you surprised at the stuff God bombarded you with that created a level of stress that you would have never seen him unless you had been bombarded with the barrage of stuff God dumped in your context? Your shout didn't come cheap. Your praise didn't come cheap. Yours was handed out in the crucible of your own suffering so that when you lift your hands you know exactly why you are.

Have you been surprised at the stuff God took you through to teach you what you had been reading all along?

Paul says, "Pray for me because the tool of my hermeneutic came to me from my disadvantage. If I had not been chained, I would not have drawn the spiritual parallels between the soldier and the saint. I had seen soldiers before, but I hadn't seen them through the lenses of my spiritual hermeneutic. Looking at the soldier, I saw some things. The belt that is truth. The shield that is faith. The sword that is my close dagger combat weapon. Shoes, that's when I nail myself down on my convictions based on the gospel. Helmet, that is to protect the control center of the mind. Prayer, so I can see things as God sees them. I wouldn't' have seen that stuff If I were sitting in the king's palace. I wouldn't have seen that if I were in the temple. I couldn't have seen that hanging with the Pharisees or Sadducees. I saw what I saw because I was chained to the guard. I didn't like it when I was chained but when I saw the armor I was able to say put on the whole armor of guard that you may be able to stand against the wiles of the devil." The things you're going through might be because God wants to pour so much into you that He is making you go through something that's really heavy because you have some heavy stuff that you need to share when you come up out of it.

Thirdly, Paul says, "Pray for me because when it's my turn I want to be bold." Some scholars suggest that when Paul says, "pray that I be fearless" that he is not talking about being bold because he is chained to the soldier. Scholars suggests that what Paul is suggesting is that there comes a time where being chained to this soldier is going to necessitate that he stand before Caesar. At that point in history, Caesar was considered one of the most powerful men in creation. Paul is saying, "Pray for me because when it's my turn to stand before Caesar, I don't want to be fearful. I want to be bold. When they walk me in and Caesar looks me in my eyes, attempting to intimidate the man of God and he asks me, 'What do you have to say for yourself?' Pray that I am fearless and point my prophetic finger in his face and say, "Caesar, you are on the throne, but Jesus is still Lord." And no matter what may come, pray that I stand there and remain bold as I declare the unsearchable riches of the kingdom of God."

We have to be bold enough in our contextual context to tell people that it is Jesus that makes a difference in a person's life. When people ask you what's the difference, tell them, "It's because I'm saved." You didn't really get saved the day you asked Jesus to come into your heart. You got saved a whole lot before that. One theologian was asked by a group when was the date he got saved. They were expecting him to give a specific day and time. Instead he said, "I didn't get saved on a specific date that I can remember. I got saved 2000 years ago on a hill called Calvary."

TEN:

LIVING TO ENCOURAGE OTHERS

Ephesians 6:21-24

"²¹Tychicus, the dear brother and faithful servant in the Lord, will tell you everything, so that you also may know how I am and what I am doing. ²²I am sending him to you for this very purpose, that you may know how we are, and that he may encourage you. ²³Peace to the brothers and sisters, and love with faith from God the Father and the Lord Jesus Christ. ²⁴Grace to all who love our Lord Jesus Christ with an undying love." (NIV)

LIVING TO ENCOURAGE SOMEBODY

The question that remains at this stage in the book is: What would make Paul think that his life and story is encouraging at all? After all, he is in prison in Rome. What would make us want to follow in his example, right? In his letter to us, he predominantly references a fight in which people of faith are engaged against an enemy that is attempting to stop the forward progression of the Christian message. Paul writes this letter in a season of extreme persecution, and he writes it for those who have committed their lives to following the executed "zealot" believed by many to be a messiah, who happens to be named Jesus. However, Paul sees his story as having the capacity to encourage those who would hear it, regardless of his imprisoned location, his pending execution, or the current persecution to which he and the saints are subjected. He writes, as he closes his letter, to the saints in Ephesus these words, "Tychicus, the dear brother and faithful servant in the Lord, will tell you everything, so that you also may know how I am and what I am doing. I am sending him to you for this very purpose, that you may know how we are, and that he may encourage you. Peace to the brothers and sisters, and love with faith from God the Father and the Lord Jesus Christ. Grace to all who love our Lord Jesus Christ with an undying love." What struck me is this one line, "I am sending him to you for this very purpose, that you may know how we are, and that he may encourage you." Paul sees his life and his conditions as having content that would encourage somebody else.

Let's quickly remind ourselves here that we are not talking about Paul sitting in some plush palace, sipping tea with mint. Paul is in prison, waiting to stand before Caesar, no doubt to be put to death. He is living in a time of extreme persecution being inflicted upon those who are bold enough to call on the name of Jesus. Paul says, "I am sending an Asiatic servant of the Lord to tell you how I am doing, what I've been up to, because I know my story will be an encouragement to the saints." Paul is suggesting that this is certainly a lesson to all of us about one of the purposes of God for our lives. God has certainly claimed and redeemed us to live to bring Him glory. Thank God He redeemed us. He has also given us the presence of the Spirit, the assurance of answered prayer, and the guidance of His word so that we might be an encouragement to each other. The angle that Paul's words bring to this consideration is this: You can be an encouragement to somebody else regardless of your personal trials, your present place, and even your private pressures. You can be an encouragement to others despite your own crisis, your overwhelming circumstances, or what for you sometimes are overbearing calamities. In fact, many times, it is those who have been through a lot who carry the most weight with people regarding advice because they have been through so much. We must all remember this as we go through our lives, challenging ourselves and making mistakes or enjoying successes. It is what we learn from our lives that we impart onto others—even in times of strife and difficulty. This lesson is hit home for us here with Paul.

It's easy to keep ourselves absent from seeing our lives as having anything encouraging to provide someone else when we are going in circles ourselves or trying to figure out our challenges. Many great mentors never offer their willingness to serve; great people of resource never willing to share, to speak up, or to show up at all simply because, in the moments of challenge, they don't realize that they are truly living examples for what to do in certain situations. Paul helps us to know that it's never your position, your pressure, your problems, or your predicaments that determine exclusively whether you can be an encouragement to somebody else. He shows us that it is OK to step out of our own situations and provide guidance based on our challenges or information based on what we know is right and good—the correct path, if you will—to success, happiness, or whatever our mentees may be seeking. Remember, he tells us and shows us that it is not position, problems, pressure, or predicaments in life that provide guidance and good examples; it is the capacity, the space, the faith you have given to God in your life so that God might show Himself through you and to reach others through you. God can get to anybody so that he or she might see Him through you, as long as you are faithfully open to letting Him reach somebody through you, at all times and in all circumstances. And, truly, for those of us who question our abilities to lead or to teach, we should take this to heart and realize that, daily, we have a lot to offer, especially with our armor of God and our prayer life. After all, strong faith brings about strong conviction and forward motion.

God can get to anybody so that he or she might see Him through you, as long as you are faithfully open to letting Him reach somebody through you, at all times and in all circumstances.

Paul sees his life and his condition as having content that would encourage somebody else. He provides the example and details it in his letter for a couple of reasons. First, Paul has learned how to be fruitful where he is planted. Notice that Paul is not trying to be planted where he thinks he can be fruitful. Instead, Paul is being fruitful where he is planted. He is in prison in Rome. He is chained to a soldier. Eventually, he will face Caesar, potentially face execution, remain restricted in mobility, and stay confined in a particular context. Despite these sad and bleak conditions, Paul is being productive from where he is. He's being productive in the work of ministry and absorbing the value of where he is and he has learned how to identify from where he is the substance that could encourage somebody else.

You are living a life that can so strongly encourage someone else, but you will only begin to see it, you will only begin to accept it, you will only begin to appreciate it when you learn how to be fruitful where you are planted. You don't have to like where you are planted; you just need to be fruitful where you are planted. The condition of a place is not as important as the condition of your spirit in that place. In fact, if you take a right spirit into a messed up place, your right spirit will turn a messed up place into a purposed place, and even if nobody else around you gets anything out of it, you'll walk away from it stronger than you were when you entered it. Truthfully, though, most people, as I said, will draw inspiration from others, and imagine what a story it would be if you could provide an example of when you had to endure a messy, terrible, negative place, yet got so much from the experience there or took away a whole new perspective, following, success story, or more.

A hungry spirit for God gets fed wherever. A person who is desperate to see God can see God wherever. A person bent on hearing God can hear God wherever. Peruse the biblical characters and see how they received their callings, or received God's message, or had their minds fixed, and their ministries empowered. You will discover that all of them received God's calling, or received God's message, or had their minds fixed and their ministries shaped in some strange, unattractive, uncomfortable, uneasy, restrictive, confining places. Yet, from these places, they learned how to discipline themselves, and they came out seeing God, sensing God, sharing with God, and saying what God instructed them to say. These are people who heard God, saw God, felt God, and sensed God—in caves, hillsides, prisons, pits, and shipwrecks—through sicknesses, mountains, deserts, captivity, graveyards—and over tree limbs, rooftops, and crosses—and after divorces, and throughout sickness, and heartache, and pain, and setback, and abuse. I don't care what your place is—when you are determined to be faithful to God—if you go in hungry to receive from God, the place is secondary, the relationship is primary, and you ignore where you are. You just become focused on what God is trying to say to you, no matter where you are.

A hungry spirit for God gets fed wherever.

Do you know how many productive, powerful, and prosperous people are going to emerge out of this global economic crisis we are living in? The folks who become productive, powerful, and prosperous won't be those who are standing around concentrating on how bad the place is right now. It will be the people who are determined that God can be seen in the darkness. Just because the economy is crunching and squeezing the American culture, there are still opportunities for people who are hungry to get on the other side of it and to be positioned just right when it is all over. Do you think that God allowed the economy to become so tight because He hates you? God allowed the economy to shrink so that people who could not participate when it was larger get a chance to participate right now. God is trying to show you that some stuff that happens is not for you to stand in that place and join the crowd of skeptics and critics, complaining about how bad it is. In fact, the opposite is often true; God put you there to show you where fresh opportunity is and somebody ought to be saying, "Speak Lord, for thy servant heareth." Just as I said before, from that "messed up" place, there is so much that can happen. I tell people all the time that beyond just the song in you today to get through the tough times is also a speech for someone else, and from that, there's a sermon meant to be heard. Beyond all that you can imagine, there is a book inside you—or a poem or a play or a new business. Miracles, breakthroughs, and advancements in all aspects of life often come from being down or in a place that does not seem right to you. When you have faith in God, and you have faith in yourself, you can take Paul's attitude and use the armor, use the prayer, and tap into your reserves to become who God intended you to be. It doesn't matter where you are. You have to look for God and learn to be fruitful from where you are planted.

In our text, Paul sees his life and circumstances as having content that would encourage somebody else because he disciplined himself to be fruitful where he was planted. Paul sees his life and circumstances as having content that would encourage somebody else because he accepted the role in universal interconnectedness. Paul doesn't lose sight of his responsibility to interpret his own life, not just for what it means for him, but he accepts responsibility for interpreting his own life in such a way, that he, through his own story, can be an encouragement to somebody else. Paul, apostle and founder of churches, commissioned preachers and shared the Gospel. If anybody shouldn't be in prison, it's Paul.

Given all this, you and I would understand if Paul had pointed his finger in God's face and said, "Is this how You treat the faithful? You let me be locked up, chained to a soldier?" God says, "Yes, because there are some places where interpretive value is only in that place. You can't see me like I want to show me anyplace else but there. There are some other people who are going through some things and need your word from the place where I have planted you." Instead, Paul says, "I got it. So instead of sitting in prison, mad that I'm chained to soldier, upset theologically because God is letting the righteous suffer—instead, let me start looking around in the place where I am and interpret what God wants to use to encourage somebody else." Paul says, "I see it. Helmet—that's salvation. Breastplate—that's righteousness. Shield—that's faith. Sword—that's the Spirit. Belt—that's truth. Shoes—that are to be nailed down on the Gospel." He wouldn't have learned that sitting on the beach. He got that sitting in prison. God has you going through some stuff because He's trying to give you something to share when you come through it. Everybody can't get where they are going on flowery beds of ease. Somebody has got to stand up and say, "In spite of it all, God can get Glory out of my life." Aren't you glad that instead of God making you live stuck in the spot where you wish you could get out of, you saw Him in it, so when you came out of it you could take somebody by the hand and say, "You're going to make it through! You are coming out! You're getting over! I don't care how bad it is. God's got a purpose and God's got a reason!"

God has you going through some stuff because He's trying to give you something to share when you come through it.

They were debating whether First Lady Michelle Obama should be officially named as an Ambassador of Good Will. One news commentator, giving her opinion, said she didn't think that was necessary because all First Ladies are Ambassadors of Good Will anyway. I thought to myself; that's absolutely right. Then, I thought how many of us Christians have to wake up and have to make a choice not to be mean and nasty for a day? How many have to make a choice that they will speak to people today—that they will smile at someone today? The truth of the matter is, as Christians, we ought to be encouragers by nature. We ought to be encouragers all the time. Nobody should have to do something for you to get encouragement from you. Your questions should be: "How will the choice I make—how will the place I walk in—how will the things I think—and how will the things I release from my mouth be a source of encouragement to other people?" I know I have a right to destroy, and I have a right to lash out. I even have a right to get back at someone or something, and I have a right to severely hurt when I've been hurt, but how do I interpret my options in such a way that, when it's all said and done, somebody else has been encouraged by the way I've walked in this place?

Nobody should have to do something for you to get encouragement from you.

I'm not telling you all that you should ignore your pain. I'm not suggesting to you that you try to bypass your pressure. I'm not trying to tell you to walk around as if you don't have any problems. What I am suggesting is that you have a larger spiritual obligation, and your obligation is to never go through something without getting something out of it that can encourage somebody else. You can't quit. You can't be exempt. You've got to go through. You are in that place, and you're responsible in that place for getting something out of it that can lift somebody else. We get this honestly because encouragement is in our blood, literally. We celebrate the shed blood of a risen savior. If He had not shed his blood you and I would not be here. That blood will never lose its power. We celebrate a Christ who learned how to be fruitful where He was planted.

FIFTH INSTALLMENT:

A TESTIMONIAL TO THE ARMOR OF GOD

Being an ambassador to all and living to encourage others are heady topics on which to end this book. I believe, however, that these are actually the easiest concepts in this book for you, as readers, to grasp. Sometimes, it is hard to understand how using your Armor of God to ward off attacks from others and from forces that might oppose or threaten your faith works. It takes effort to tap into all of these bits of advice that Paul gave us—to remember to wear our faith boldly and to act when we feel it is appropriate. It is easier, as Christians with an inherent sense of duty to others, to live God's Word—to talk about your faith—and to give back when you can.

We all have our moments of reflection in life. They occur when we reach a milestone in life—hit a major birthday or run a marathon—even get a big promotion. They occur, too, when our kids render us sentimental and nostalgic with shows at the holidays—gifts out of nowhere—their own milestones that remind us how fast time passes, etc. We reflect at the holidays, when there is a death in the family, when we come out of difficult time in life and into the sunshine of new hope. Do we ever take a moment in our busy days, however, to reflect on our life, our day, or our faith?

I can answer that for all of us. We don't. Hopefully, however, this book helped you all examine your faith and your commitment to defending it. I'm hoping, too, that it has also made you more aware of the threats that often do come our way and throw us off track. Life could be successful and stress-free and constantly fulfilling if we just learn—or, more to the point—stay aware—of the forces out there that can cause us to stray from a disciplined, faithful, and, ultimately, successful life. And…back to reflection…I am hoping this book served as a reflective tool for you. By design, I wanted everyone to look inside and to re-evaluate what was important in life—what would we protect—what do we protect—and what do we need to protect?

As I said earlier, I do think it is easy for us as Christians to, at least, have being an ambassador of our faith or encouraging others to do the same on our radar. What is interesting, however, is gauging how often we all act on those impulses or obligations. Often, this reaching out or being an ambassador comes in spurts—again, at the holidays when it is time to feed the hungry and buy toys for children who don't have much under their tree at Christmas. Do we keep this sense of giving and reaching out alive during the year, however? Should we?

Of course we should. We should live our daily lives in faith, love, and charity. We should abide by the "Golden Rule" to treat others as we want to be treated. And, we should always remember to wear our Armor of God—and remain ambassadors to the faith. If anything, simply protecting our lives and what is important to us should motivate us. Giving back to others, as I alluded to before, should be inherently obvious to us as Christians. In reflecting on this book, I want you all to take away a sense of strength and a sense of duty. We are the faces of the Armor of God; now go forward and live the life you were meant to live!

ABOUT THE AUTHOR

A native of Baltimore, Maryland, Dr. William H. Curtis accepted the call to ministry at the age of 17. For seven years, he served as the Senior Pastor at Shiloh Baptist Church in York, PA; however, since 1997, he has served as the Senior Pastor at Mount Ararat Baptist Church in Pittsburgh, PA.

Mount Ararat Baptist Church is a large urban ministry and ministers to more than 10,000 members in the community, providing four well attended weekend services. Under the ministry of Dr. Curtis, Mt. Ararat has grown exponentially, and his guidance has lead to several landmark events and successes, including the formation of a Community Development Corporation to minister to the greater Pittsburgh area, and the liquidation of the church mortgage in a one-day "Harvest Sunday" offering. Additionally, he implemented a Community Tithe Program, which returns over ten percent of the congregation's weekly offerings to the community.

Dr. Curtis is a highly popular and widely sought after speaker. In addition to his responsibilities at Mount Ararat, he is an instructor at the United Theological Seminary and has graduated several groups of doctoral students there, and he has recently preached the Word of God at over 50 Revivals all over the United States. Dr. Curtis also lends his support to a number of corporate and independent community endeavors. He is co-owner of The Church Online, a successful technology and full-service marketing firm that provides top of the line services to ministries all over the world.

Dr. Curtis serves as a Board Member for Amachi Pittsburgh, a faith-based organization focused on assisting children of incarcerated parents, and he is a member of the Omega Psi Phi Fraternity. Dr. Curtis has also served on the Board of the Pittsburgh Sports and Exhibition Authority; the Board of the Pittsburgh Theological Seminary; the Board of Trustees of The Ellis School, a preparatory school for girls; the Board of Trustees of the Interdenominational Theological Center; and the Baptist School of Theology. In addition to his many board appointments, he served as President of the highly popular Hampton University Minister's Conference from 2007–2011.

Dr. Curtis has been the recipient of numerous honors and awards. In 2009, he was inducted into the Martin Luther King Jr. Board of Preachers of Morehouse College. In the spring of 2010, Dr. Curtis moved from the speaking arena into the publishing arena with his first book, "FAITH: Learning to Live Without Fear," which is currently in its fourth printing. "Dressed for Victory: Putting On the Full Armor of God" is his second book.

ABOUT THE AUTHOR

Dr. Curtis holds a Bachelor of Arts Degree in Religious Studies and Philosophy from Morgan State University, a Master of Divinity Degree from Howard University School of Divinity, and a Doctor of Ministry Degree from United Theological Seminary in Dayton, Ohio.

Dr. Curtis is married to the former Christine Y. Richardson, and they are the proud parents of one lovely daughter, Houston.